AMERICA'S
TEST KITCHEN

Instant Pot® ACE BLENDER COOKBOOK

FOOLPROOF RECIPES FOR THE BLENDER THAT ALSO COOKS

AMERICA'S TEST KITCHEN

Instant Pot® and associated logos are owned by Instant Brands Inc. and are used under license.

The photos on pages 2 and 3 are courtesy of Instant Pot.

Library of Congress Cataloging-in-Publication Data has been applied for.

ISBN 978-1-948703-03-1

—— AMERICA'S ——
TEST KITCHEN ®

America's Test Kitchen
21 Drydock Avenue, Boston, MA 02210

Manufactured in the United States of America
10 9 8 7 6 5 4 3 2 1

Distributed by Penguin Random House
Publisher Services
Tel: 800.733.3000

PICTURED ON FRONT COVER Carrot-Ginger Soup (page 25)

PICTURED ON BACK COVER Barbecued Pork Sandwiches (page 52), Thai Shrimp Curry (page 55), Easy Ground Beef Chili (page 48), Almond Milk (page 89), Mole Chicken Tacos (page 47)

EDITORIAL DIRECTOR, BOOKS Elizabeth Carduff

EXECUTIVE EDITOR Adam Kowit

EXECUTIVE FOOD EDITOR Dan Zuccarello

RECIPE DEVELOPMENT Sandra Wu

SENIOR EDITORS Nicole Konstantinakos and Russell Selander

ASSOCIATE EDITOR Lawman Johnson

EXECUTIVE MANAGING EDITOR Debra Hudak

EDITORIAL ASSISTANT Brenna Donovan

ART DIRECTOR, BOOKS Lindsey Timko Chandler

DEPUTY ART DIRECTORS Allison Boales, Courtney Lentz, and Janet Taylor

ASSOCIATE ART DIRECTOR Katie Barranger

PHOTOGRAPHY DIRECTOR Julie Bozzo Cote

PHOTOGRAPHY PRODUCER Meredith Mulcahy

SENIOR STAFF PHOTOGRAPHER Daniel J. van Ackere

STAFF PHOTOGRAPHERS Steve Klise and Kevin White

ADDITIONAL PHOTOGRAPHY Keller + Keller and Carl Tremblay

FOOD STYLING Chantal Lambeth, Catrine Kelty, and Ashley Moore

PHOTOSHOOT KITCHEN TEAM

PHOTO TEAM AND SPECIAL EVENTS MANAGER Timothy McQuinn

LEAD TEST COOK Jessica Rudolph

ASSISTANT TEST COOKS Sarah Ewald, Jacqueline Gochenouer, and Eric Haessler

SENIOR MANAGER, PUBLISHING OPERATIONS Taylor Argenzio

IMAGING MANAGER Lauren Robbins

PRODUCTION AND IMAGING SPECIALISTS Dennis Noble, Jessica Voas, and Amanda Yong

COPY EDITOR Debra Hudak

PROOFREADER Kelly Gauthier

INDEXER Elizabeth Parson

CHIEF CREATIVE OFFICER Jack Bishop

EXECUTIVE EDITORIAL DIRECTORS Julia Collin Davison and Bridget Lancaster

CONTENTS

WELCOME TO AMERICA'S TEST KITCHEN

This book has been tested, written, and edited by the folks at America's Test Kitchen. Located in Boston's Seaport District in the historic Innovation and Design Building, it features 15,000 square feet of kitchen space including multiple photography and video studios. It is the home of *Cook's Illustrated* magazine and *Cook's Country* magazine and is the workday destination for more than 60 test cooks, editors, and cookware specialists. Our mission is to test recipes over and over again until we understand how and why they work and until we arrive at the best version.

We start the process of testing a recipe with a complete lack of preconceptions, which means that we accept no claim, no technique, and no recipe at face value. We simply assemble as many variations as possible, test a half-dozen of the most promising, and taste the results blind. We then construct our own recipe and continue to test it, varying ingredients, techniques, and cooking times until we reach a consensus. As we like to say in the test kitchen, "We make the mistakes so you don't have to." The result, we hope, is the best version of a particular recipe, but we realize that only you can be the final judge of our success (or failure). We use the same rigorous approach when we test equipment and taste ingredients.

All of this would not be possible without a belief that good cooking, much like good music, is based on a foundation of objective technique. Some people like spicy foods and others don't, but there is a right way to sauté, there is a best way to cook a pot roast, and there are measurable scientific principles involved in producing perfectly beaten, stable egg whites. Our ultimate goal is to investigate the fundamental principles of cooking to give you the techniques, tools, and ingredients you need to become a better cook. It is as simple as that.

To see what goes on behind the scenes at America's Test Kitchen, check out our social media channels for kitchen snapshots, exclusive content, video tips, and much more. You can watch us work (in our actual test kitchen) by tuning in to *America's Test Kitchen* or *Cook's Country* on public television or on our websites. Listen in to test kitchen experts on public radio (SplendidTable.org) to hear insights that illuminate the truth about real home cooking. Want to hone your cooking skills or finally learn how to bake—with an America's Test Kitchen test cook? Enroll in one of our online cooking classes. However you choose to visit us, we welcome you into our kitchen, where you can stand by our side as we test our way to the best recipes in America.

facebook.com/AmericasTestKitchen
twitter.com/TestKitchen
youtube.com/AmericasTestKitchen
instagram.com/TestKitchen
pinterest.com/TestKitchen

AmericasTestKitchen.com
CooksIllustrated.com
CooksCountry.com
OnlineCookingSchool.com

INTRODUCTION

Here in the test kitchen we are always on the lookout for new appliances that can make cooking better or easier. So when Instant Pot came out with its Ace Multi-Use Cooking and Beverage Blender, we were intrigued to say the least. Did it work? And what, exactly, could you make using a blender that cooks? We were in uncharted territory.

As the blogosphere lit up with reviews and a clamoring for recipes beyond the usual smoothies, we put this blender through its paces. We found much to like about it (see page 5), but realizing the full potential of this cutting-edge device is not intuitive. The Ace blender has eight discrete "smart" functions (four cold and four hot), but it is the two soup programs (chunky and creamy), which combine chopping, pureeing, or mixing with heating, that truly set this device apart from other blenders on the market. Ultimately it was the power of these two functions that convinced us that this was an appliance worthy of space in a home kitchen.

We expected recipe development to be a challenge because, as we have learned over the years with our slow cooker, pressure cooker, and air fryer books, we needed to develop recipes designed JUST for this appliance. And sometimes we found that we needed to hack the device to get the results we really wanted. This turned out to be especially true with the Ace blender. Interrupting preset programs turned out to be the key to success in many recipes in the book.

As we experimented in the test kitchen, we learned simple tricks for developing flavor without browning (hint: use the microwave to bloom spices and soften aromatics), reducing ingredient prep, and using convenience products in ways that didn't compromise the quality of the finished dish. This book delivers 75 foolproof recipes you'll really want to make at home—many of which will undoubtedly seem surprising.

Witness Mole Chicken Tacos (a super-charged mole sauce meets tender chicken), Zoodles Puttanesca (zucchini noodles cook right in our from-scratch sauce), and Easy Ground Beef Chili (we make a chili base in the blender and add chunks of ground meat for a remarkably good dinner in record time). There are surprisingly sophisticated recipes here too, like Thai Shrimp Curry and Parmesan Farrotto. And none of the recipes in this book use the stovetop—if you are trying to make dinner in your blender, the last thing you want to do is dirty a skillet.

At the end of our recipe development process, we were converts to using a blender that could cook a meal and handle the usual blender tasks (yes, it makes nice smoothies). In the pages that follow, you will learn exactly how to use the Instant Pot Ace Multi-Use Cooking and Beverage Blender along with the tips, techniques, and discoveries that enabled the test kitchen to make the most of it.

GETTING TO KNOW THE ACE BLENDER

The Ace Multi-Use Cooking and Beverage Blender has eight smart touch programs: four cold blending programs (Smoothie, Crushed Ice, Ice Cream, and Nut/Oat Milk) and four hot (Purée, Soy Milk, Rice Milk, and Soup) as well as multiple other features. Note that programs with two dots on the blender panel indicate that you can toggle between two options, i.e., chunky versus creamy for style of soup, white versus brown when making rice milk, and soft versus hard when pureeing vegetables or fruit. This overview gives you the basics while the manual that comes with the blender has further detailed information that you may find helpful.

THE LID

The blender has a substantial lid with a safety lock, a lid brace, and a black silicone seal. It also has a lid cap that clicks into place and can be replaced with the food tamper for certain applications. It was a bit unnerving for us at first to watch contents boiling vigorously and moving up and down in the blender jar when we weren't keeping our hands on the lid with a kitchen towel as we usually do when pureeing hot contents in a regular blender. But this blender is designed for these hot functions and we never had any issues with the lid coming loose. You can walk away without fear.

THE GLASS PITCHER

The heavy-duty, 60-ounce tempered glass pitcher is what allows for simultaneous boiling and blending. It weighs 5½ pounds and has a capacity of 54 ounces for cold contents and a maximum safe capacity of 48 ounces for hot contents. Because the heating element and eight stainless-steel blades are built into the bottom of the pitcher and not removable, the pitcher cannot be submerged in water when cleaning it or put in the dishwasher. The pitcher fits easily into place in the base of the blender if you align the position indicator (white triangle) on the bottom of the pitcher with the triangle on the base. When properly aligned, the handle will point to the right. Note that the blender will not turn on until the base and glass pitcher are properly connected.

THE BASE AND CONTROL PANEL

The large and clearly labeled base has 14 buttons, three of which are simply blending speeds related to the basic blend function. One of the most striking features of this blender is that it has two LED panels: one tracks the time of the selected preset function, and the other tracks the real-time rising temperature when using a hot function. Although you cannot preset the temperature, it is useful to see it because the hot functions don't start timing until the temperature reaches the boiling point. (The amount of time that it takes for the contents to reach the target temperature varies depending on the amount of liquid and the amount and size of other ingredients in the blender.) When it does, the preset timing for the function in use will start counting down. When the cycle is complete, the blender will beep loudly 10 times and the display will read "done."

ACCESSORIES

The accessories that come with the blender include a very helpful food tamper, which replaces the lid cap and is useful in both main dishes that require regular stirring and smoothies, a 150mL/5oz measuring cup, a cleaning brush, and a food-safe strainer bag with drawstring, which can be used when making alternative milks (though we found that using a cheesecloth-lined strainer offered an equally user-friendly and practical straining alternative).

Avoiding Scorching

Given that this is a blender that heats food to the boiling point, it is hard to avoid the fact that some ingredients, including those with high sugar or high fat content, will stick to the metal plate and potentially make a bit of a mess. This is especially true with canned tomato products. When possible we tried to thin our sauces with broth to prevent scorching but not so much so as to compromise the final texture.

How to Clean Your Ace Blender

In general, it is easy to clean the blender by using a bottle or dishwashing brush and soapy water. Sometimes, if there is some stuck-on food or scorched food on the bottom, you will want to run the Pulse/Clean function. To use the function, simply fill the pitcher with 34 ounces of hot water and press the button. Discard the water after it has run and fill again adding a little soap this time and run the program again. Rinse with warm water to finish.

A CLOSER LOOK AT THE CONTROL PANEL

SMOOTHIE

This preset is for making any type of smoothie using fresh or frozen fruit, berries, seeds, yogurt, greens, and more. It runs for 1 minute and 38 seconds.

PURÉE

This preset is designed to puree softened or partially cooked vegetables for side dishes or baby food. It has two options: one for hard vegetables like carrots, cauliflower, and butternut squash (2 minutes 56 seconds) and another for soft fruits and vegetables like tomatoes and spinach (24 seconds).

CRUSHED ICE

The Ace excels at crushing ice; this is a 30-second program.

ICE CREAM (AND SORBET)

There are two ways to make ice cream in the Ace blender. One is to make a no-churn style where you create a whipped base in the blender that once frozen is scoopable. The second is to freeze fruit, as we do with our Banana Ice Cream, then process it with cream and other ingredients and freeze it. We also use this function to make sorbet; we put a flavorful liquid or juice in ice cube trays, freeze it, then process it with other ingredients using the ice cream function.

ALTERNATIVE MILK FUNCTIONS

There are three buttons with presets for making plant-based milk: Soy, Rice (this has separate choices for white and brown rice milk), and Nut/Oat milk. The soy and rice milk programs are hot blending programs. For more recipe-specific details about making these milks, see page 9.

SOUP FUNCTIONS

The Soup function offers two options: The first option that appears when you press the button is for making chunky soups. The blending mechanism is disabled in this preset program so it allows you to make cohesive soups with a chunkier texture. This function runs for 20 minutes after the contents have reached the boiling point. Option 2 is for making creamy soups and has a powerful blending capacity. This function runs for 22 minutes and 44 seconds after it reaches the boiling point. Note that the functions are numbered and do not say chunky or creamy. Our recipes are very clear about which function to choose. Note that these programs start with very gentle blending, and add an intermittent quick-stir motion to agitate the food contents throughout the program. The creamy soup function starts more intense blending in the last minutes of the cycle.

MANUAL BLENDING PROGRAMS

Below the temperature block you will see the standard manual blending programs of low, medium, and high speeds. The blender will beep 3 times 5 seconds after you select your desired speed and then start blending. You can change the speed at any time without interrupting the cycle.

PAUSE BUTTON

This will stop the blending program and is useful when you want to add ingredients mid-program, which we often do when making soups and other hot dishes. To resume just press the button a second time.

CANCEL BUTTON

This stops the blending program at any time, in which case the blender reverts to a standby mode and the panel displays OFF.

PULSE/CLEAN BUTTON

This function, with its short bursts of blending, breaks up larger chunks of food or can be used for cleaning.

EVALUATING THE ACE BLENDER

We've tested a lot of blenders over the years and quite a few of them promised to make hot soup—but none delivered. That is because they all relied on friction from their spinning blades to heat the food, delivering lukewarm soup at best. So we were intrigued when Instant Pot, the maker of the incredibly popular multicooker, launched the Ace, a blender that has a built-in heating element.

To see how well the Ace worked, we bought copies and used them to make smoothies, mayonnaise, crushed ice, and almond milk, in addition to several soups that we made right in the blender jar, adding raw ingredients like chunks of carrot, cauliflower florets, and asparagus stems.

The Ace performed well in our tests, most notably the soups. It has two preset functions: after preheating (which takes roughly 5 to 20 minutes, depending on the contents), one cooks for 20 minutes and blends gently at the end for a chunky soup, and the other cooks for 22 minutes and 44 seconds and blends vigorously at the end for a smooth soup. The model successfully cooked and blended raw ingredients into piping hot soup, something we've never seen a blender do before.

The control panel is quite busy (sporting buttons for no less than three different kinds of milk, for example), but easy enough to use.

The blender jar is glass, which is a plus for those avoiding plastic but a downside for maneuverability: at 5½ pounds it was heavy to pour from. Also, you can't submerge the jar because the bottom houses the heating element and the blades, which makes cleaning a bit cumbersome. However, we understand that future models of the Ace blender will have detachable blades, making it easier to clean. Instant Pot recommends blending soap and water in the jar to clean it, but this doesn't get the top, so you have to finish washing it by hand, being careful to keep the bottom dry.

Do You Have a Different Model?
Instant Pot updates its appliances frequently, and we stay on top of these changes on our website when it relates to previous testings and our books. If you have a different model of the Ace blender, we encourage you to visit our website *www.americastestkitchen.com/ aceblenderbook* for helpful tutorials and other information that were not available to us at the time this book went to press.

TEST KITCHEN TIPS AND DISCOVERIES

While developing recipes for this book we learned a few things about how to get the best results using the Ace blender and, in particular, how to adapt traditional recipes and existing blender recipes to work best using it. Here's what we learned.

USING THE SOUP FUNCTION (AND GOING BEYOND JUST SOUP)

The convenience of the Soup function, with its creamy and chunky soup preset programs, really won us over. We found that we could create silky-smooth creamy soups with very little prep, and we loved that we could simply pour them out of the glass pitcher and into our bowls. And the chunky function gave us a bit more control, which allowed us to push the limits of the blender to make curries, a stir-fry, chili, chunky soup bases, and even cook tiny meatballs in our soup. The blender basically heats, mixes, and stirs, and heats some more, rather like what

happens when you make some soup on the stovetop by hand. Only here it happens with a touch of a button. At first, we were nervous watching soup boil in a glass blender, especially when parts of the cycle appeared to be aggressively mixing and boiling the ingredients at once. We watched this process unfold before us with great fascination as the weeks in the test kitchen went by. And we were impressed by both the quality and convenience of the recipes we could make. But there were a few tricks and hacks that we came to rely on to achieve the best results.

INGREDIENT PREP: FORGET THE NORMAL RULES

For lush and creamy soups, we found that we could spare our hands a little knife work and cut ingredients into chunks. The powerful heating and blending program did the rest of the work for us perfectly. For instance, for our Carrot-Ginger Soup, we cut the carrots into 1½-inch pieces, a big timesaver given that we had more than a pound of carrots to peel and cut. Then we simply tossed in a whole peeled garlic clove and a chunk of peeled ginger—no tedious mincing required. But for chunkier soups and other types of recipes, like Classic Chicken Noodle Soup and Chicken Cacciatore, we found that we had to cut the ingredients to the size we wanted them to be in the final dish. For Classic Chicken Noodle Soup, we cut the carrots, onion, and celery into ¾-inch pieces for an appealingly hearty dish. Cut any larger they would have led to a soup that was out of balance. For Chicken Cacciatore, we cut mushrooms into quarters to give the dish texture and heft, and we cut roasted red peppers into ½-inch-thick strips for the same reason. But we minced the garlic since the chunky soup function wouldn't break it down enough.

USE THE MICROWAVE (SOMETIMES)

Perhaps the biggest challenge when making recipes in the Ace blender is that there is no way to brown in it to build flavor, so we needed to find a work-around. Since using a skillet was out of the question, we turned to a trick we discovered when using a slow cooker: bloom spices and aromatics in the microwave with a little oil and other flavor-building ingredients like tomato paste. It takes just minutes and in some recipes made a big difference. We also turned to the microwave when we needed to soften ingredients, as we did when making Sweet and Sour Beef with Shiitakes and Bell Pepper. Because we were essentially building a stir-fry and its sauce in the blender, we wanted to add partially cooked vegetables to the sauce toward the end of the cycle without overcooking them; the micro-wave cooked the mushrooms and the bell pepper strips to just the right crisp-tenderness. For our Indian Vegetable Curry, we both built flavor and softened the cauliflower and potatoes at once using the microwave; a potent mix of tomato paste, curry powder, onion, garlic, and ginger came to life in the microwave and infused our curry with great depth of flavor.

STAGGER THE ADDITION OF INGREDIENTS

When re-creating a traditional main dish using the Ace blender, you cannot just dump all the ingredients into the glass jar and press the chunky soup preset button. The first step is always to create either a brothy flavor base or creamy or chunky base to which you can add other ingredients during the cycle. Our recipes specify the exact timing for this so all you need to do is watch the clock on the LED screen on the blender. For Spaghetti and Meatball Soup, we pause the chunky soup program 12 minutes before it is completed and add the ditalini and the tiny meatballs so they will cook through perfectly. (No one will suspect this dish came together in a blender.)

HACK THE FUNCTIONS

When pushing the limits of what this blender could do, we needed a few tricks. Take beef chili. Normally you'd create a thick tomatoey base for chili on the stovetop by simmering it for a while. But in a blender that just won't happen. So we created a concentrated base with just the right texture by grinding down a can of whole peeled tomatoes with ½ cup chicken broth using the medium blending speed. We also used the chunky soup function after adding the beans and finished our chili by stirring in the raw ground beef pieces 15 minutes before the cycle ended. There are quite a few recipes in the book where one of the blending functions, in conjunction with the chunky soup function, delivered great results.

HOW AND WHEN TO USE CONVENIENCE PRODUCTS

We realize that if you are making a meal in the blender, you are looking for an easier option—not a recipe with a laundry list of ingredients and a ton of prep work. So we had to balance flavor and quality with convenience. Some shortcuts like using rotisserie chicken (or leftover cooked chicken) or precooked pasta and rice seemed easy enough and the results were great. In other cases we chose to use ingredients like raw shrimp, which we preferred to precooked in terms of quality. Instead of buying precooked shredded pork for our Barbecued Pork Sandwiches, we used pork tenderloin, which was easy enough to slice thinly and add to the zesty sauce.

MAKING PLANT-BASED MILKS

For anyone interested in alternative milks, the Ace blender holds a lot of appeal because you can make a variety of milks using the presets and our recipes. What's great about making the milks from scratch is that they are free of additives like thickeners, you can control the amount of sugar added, and they are easy to make and economical. Two of the milks use a hot function: soy milk and rice milk. All of the milks require straining at the end. The blender comes with a small strainer bag made of finely woven material. We found it to be a bit easier to line a fine-mesh strainer with cheesecloth and set it over a large measuring cup. The additional surface area of this setup made it easier to maneuver and pour a heavy glass pitcher full of milk without incident.

SMOOTHIE PERFECTION

Smoothies offer a lot of versatility when it comes to packing nutrients and flavor into a single drink. And of course there are myriad recipes out there for all sorts of smoothies. In this book you'll find a fruit-based smoothie and a greens-based one. There are two things you need to turn out a perfect smoothie: a great recipe with just the right proportion of each ingredient and a powerful blender. The Ace blender powers through frozen fruit and greens easily and its preset smoothie button ensures your drink is ultra smooth. How you layer the ingredients into the glass jar can make a difference. The best way, starting at the base, is: liquids, protein powder and sweetener, leafy greens, soft ingredients (yogurt, avocado, nut butter, etc.), fresh fruit, nuts and seeds, and frozen fruit and ice cubes (if using).

Making Desserts in the Ace Blender

You can make a variety of very appealing treats easily with this blender. First, it is possible to make no-churn ice cream that starts with a whipped cream base, a banana ice cream, and a variety of grown-up sorbets using the ice cream function (though there is a freezing step involved in each of these recipes to deliver scoopable results). Chocolate mousse is easy to whip up using the microwave and the blending function. See the No-Fuss Desserts and Frozen Treats chapter for these recipes and more.

PERFECT SOUPS WITHOUT THE STOVETOP

CLASSIC CHICKEN NOODLE SOUP

SERVES 2 TO 4

TOTAL TIME
45 minutes

- 3 **cups chicken broth**

- 1 **small onion, cut into ¾-inch pieces**

- 2 **carrots, peeled and cut into ¾-inch pieces**

- 1 **celery rib, cut into ¾-inch pieces**

- 1 **garlic clove, minced**

- 1 **teaspoon minced fresh thyme or ¼ teaspoon dried**

- ½ **teaspoon table salt**

- ¼ **teaspoon pepper**

- 1½ **cups shredded cooked chicken**

- 1 **cup fully cooked pasta, such as rotini or elbow macaroni**

- ¼ **cup frozen peas**

- 1 **tablespoon minced fresh parsley**

WHY THIS RECIPE WORKS The idea of making a rich-tasting chicken noodle soup using just the Ace blender was super appealing. We wanted an aromatic-rich broth that tasted homemade with tender shreds of chicken, peas, and enough pasta to make it hearty. The key, as we quickly learned, was getting the right cut and size of the mirepoix (the onion, celery, and carrot) that gives this simple soup its backbone. Cutting these vegetables into moderately sized pieces ensured that they wouldn't fully melt into the soup, thereby making their presence known both in terms of texture and flavor. The chunky soup function on the Ace blender worked perfectly in terms of leaving bits of these vegetables intact. A clove of garlic and fresh thyme rounded out the flavors of the brothy base of our soup. We stopped the cooking cycle 2 minutes before it completed so we could add shredded cooked chicken, cooked pasta, and frozen peas, which gave all of them just enough time to heat up and mingle with the delicious broth.

1. Add broth, onion, carrots, celery, garlic, thyme, salt, and pepper to Ace blender. Lock lid in place, then select soup program 1 (for chunky soups).

2. Pause program 2 minutes before it has completed. Carefully remove lid and stir in chicken, pasta, and peas. Return lid and resume program. Once program has completed, stir in parsley and season with salt and pepper to taste. Serve.

CLASSIC CHICKEN AND RICE SOUP
Substitute 1 cup fully cooked long-grain white or brown rice for pasta.

CHICKEN AND RAMEN SOUP

SERVES 2

TOTAL TIME
45 minutes

4 cups chicken broth

3 scallions, white and
   green parts separated
   and sliced thin

1 tablespoon dry sherry
   (optional)

2 teaspoons grated
   fresh ginger

2 garlic cloves, minced

1 teaspoon soy sauce,
   plus extra as needed

1 cup shredded
   coleslaw mix

1 cup baby spinach

¾ cup shredded cooked
   chicken

1 (3-ounce) package
   ramen noodles, flavoring
   packet discarded, noodle
   bundle halved

1 teaspoon sesame oil,
   plus extra as needed

WHY THIS RECIPE WORKS Asian-style noodle soups are built around a full-flavored broth. We achieved a quick blender version by simply adding a mix of aromatics plus soy sauce and dry sherry to the blender with 4 cups of store-bought broth. After whirling around and heating up in the blender, our broth mixture was pungent and savory—the perfect broth base to which we could add convenient shredded rotisserie chicken, coleslaw mix, bright spinach, and ramen noodles. Just three minutes of cooking in the chunky soup cycle at the end was enough to warm up the chicken, cook the noodles and wilt the slaw and the spinach. All our simple and beautiful-looking soup needed to finish was a drizzle of sesame oil. To ensure the noodles cook through properly, it is important to submerge them completely in the broth before resuming the program in step 2. You can find shredded coleslaw mix in the packaged salad aisle at the grocery store.

1. Add broth, scallion whites, sherry, if using, ginger, garlic, and soy sauce to Ace blender. Lock lid in place, then select soup program 1 (for chunky soups).

2. Pause program 3 minutes before it has completed. Carefully remove lid, stir in coleslaw mix, spinach, and chicken, then completely submerge noodles in mixture. Return lid and resume program.

3. Once program has completed, stir in scallion greens and sesame oil. Season with extra soy sauce and sesame oil to taste. Using tongs, divide noodles, vegetables, and chicken evenly between serving bowls, then pour remaining soup over top. Serve immediately.

MEXICAN CHICKEN SOUP

SERVES 2 TO 4

TOTAL TIME
45 minutes

3 cups chicken broth

1 small tomato, cored
and chopped

1 small onion, cut into
¾-inch pieces

2 garlic cloves, minced

2 teaspoons tomato paste

1 teaspoon minced
canned chipotle chile
in adobo sauce

½ teaspoon ground cumin

¼ teaspoon table salt

1 cup shredded
cooked chicken

1 cup frozen corn kernels,
thawed

¾ cup canned pinto
beans, rinsed

2 tablespoons chopped
fresh cilantro

2 teaspoons lime juice,
plus lime wedges
for serving

WHY THIS RECIPE WORKS Mexican chicken soup is a richer, spicier rendition of everybody's favorite soup and is similarly easy to translate to the Ace blender given that it uses shredded cooked chicken. Tomato, corn, and beans all play a role in making this soup distinct and hearty. To make soup with a full, authentic flavor, we started by seasoning the broth base with garlic, chipotle chile, tomato paste, and cumin. Chopped tomato and onion rounded everything out. Adding the shredded chicken, corn, and beans towards the end of cooking allowed everything to heat through properly without being overly broken down. Serve with crumbled tortilla chips, diced avocado, and shredded Monterey Jack cheese, if desired.

1. Add broth, tomato, onion, garlic, tomato paste, chipotle, cumin, and salt to Ace blender. Lock lid in place, then select soup program 1 (for chunky soups).

2. Pause program 3 minutes before it has completed. Carefully remove lid and stir in chicken, corn, and beans. Return lid and resume program. Once program has completed, stir in cilantro and lime juice and season with salt and pepper to taste. Serve with lime wedges.

BEEF AND BARLEY SOUP

SERVES 2 TO 4

TOTAL TIME
50 minutes

- 4 ounces cremini mushrooms, trimmed and quartered
- 1 small onion, cut into ¾-inch pieces
- 1½ tablespoons tomato paste
- 1 tablespoon vegetable oil
- 3 garlic cloves, minced
- 1 teaspoon minced fresh thyme or ¼ teaspoon dried
- ¼ teaspoon pepper
- 3 cups beef broth
- 1 carrot, peeled and cut into ¾-inch pieces
- 1 tablespoon soy sauce
- 8 ounces top sirloin steak, trimmed and cut into ¼-inch pieces
- ¼ cup quick-cooking barley
- 2 tablespoons minced fresh parsley

WHY THIS RECIPE WORKS This soup is hearty enough for dinner, so the idea of making it in the blender held great appeal. First, we focused on building a beefy broth without browning the beef in a skillet to create a fond that would infuse the soup with flavor when deglazed. Instead we turned to a potent combo of umami-packed mushrooms and tomato paste plus onion and garlic, which we bloomed in the microwave. Our base assembled, we simply added it to the blender along with beef broth, soy sauce (a test kitchen trick for adding beefy flavor), and chopped carrot for vegetal sweetness. We selected the chunky soup program because we knew we'd want to add thinly sliced beef after the preheating phase so it would cook through but not become pulverized. We used top sirloin because it is so lean and did not make the soup greasy. For the barley, a judicious ¼ cup of quick-cooking barley fit the bill and we added it along with the beef. Be sure to use quick-cooking (sometimes labeled "quick-cooking pearled") or pre-steamed barley, which has been partially cooked during processing to reduce its cooking time.

1. Microwave mushrooms, onion, tomato paste, oil, garlic, thyme, and pepper in bowl, stirring occasionally, until vegetables are softened, about 5 minutes; transfer to Ace blender along with broth, carrot, and soy sauce. Lock lid in place, then select soup program 1 (for chunky soups).

2. Pause program once preheating ends (countdown timer will display 20 minutes). Carefully remove lid and stir in steak and barley. Return lid and resume program. Once program has completed, season with salt and pepper to taste. Sprinkle individual portions with parsley and serve.

SPAGHETTI AND MEATBALL SOUP

SERVES 2 TO 4

TOTAL TIME
50 minutes

1 small onion, cut into ¾-inch pieces

1 carrot, peeled and cut into ¾-inch pieces

1 tablespoon extra-virgin olive oil, plus extra for serving

2 garlic cloves, peeled

¾ teaspoon table salt

2 cups chicken broth, plus extra as needed

1 (14.5-ounce) can whole peeled tomatoes

6 ounces hot or sweet Italian sausage, casings removed

3 tablespoons panko bread crumbs

½ cup small pasta, such as ditalini, tubettini, or elbow macaroni

Grated Parmesan cheese

WHY THIS RECIPE WORKS This kid-friendly soup takes its inspiration from canned Spaghetti Os but is much healthier and so tasty that even adults will like it. Making it in the blender requires a two-step process: First, to create the tomatoey base we add the softened aromatics, broth, and canned whole tomatoes to the blender and puree this mixture until smooth. Second, we selected the chunky soup program to finish the soup and then poach the meatballs and pasta. These tiny meatballs boost the protein of the soup and ante up the fun factor too. And adding the pasta to the saucy base as it cooks toward the end releases its starch and gives the soup its recognizably thick consistency. To make the meatballs, we removed the casings from Italian sausage (which is nicely seasoned) and mixed the meat with panko bread crumbs so the meatballs would hold together when added to the blender. In our testing we found it best to stop the chunky soup function 12 minutes before completion to add the tiny meatballs and the small pasta. This is the perfect meal to whip up in your blender when hungry kids are waiting. Be sure to roll the sausage mixture into ¾-inch meatballs; larger meatballs will not cook through properly.

1. Microwave onion, carrot, oil, garlic, and salt in bowl, stirring occasionally, until vegetables are softened, about 5 minutes; transfer to Ace blender along with broth and tomatoes and their juice. Lock lid in place, then process on medium speed until vegetables are finely ground, about 30 seconds. Scrape down sides of blender jar. Return lid and process on high speed until smooth, about 1 minute.

2. Select soup program 1 (for chunky soups). Meanwhile, mix sausage and panko together in bowl with hands until well combined. Pinch off and roll sausage mixture into ¾-inch meatballs (you should have about 24 meatballs); transfer to plate and refrigerate until ready to use.

3. Pause program 12 minutes before it has completed. Carefully remove lid, stir in pasta, then gently nestle meatballs into soup until completely submerged. Return lid and resume program. Once program has completed, adjust soup consistency with extra broth as needed and season with salt and pepper to taste. Drizzle individual portions with extra oil and sprinkle with Parmesan cheese before serving.

CREAMY TOMATO SOUP

SERVES 2 TO 4

TOTAL TIME
50 minutes

1 small onion, cut into
   1-inch pieces

2 tablespoons tomato paste

2 tablespoons unsalted
   butter

¾ teaspoon table salt

1 (28-ounce) can whole
   peeled tomatoes

1½ cups chicken or vegetable
   broth, plus extra as
   needed

1 tablespoon packed
   brown sugar

¼ cup heavy cream

2 tablespoons minced
   fresh chives

WHY THIS RECIPE WORKS Making a deeply flavored tomato soup is hard enough on the stovetop, so making one in a blender seemed daunting. First, there was the tomatoes: fresh or canned? Second, the matter of technique: how to add flavor and texture to the soup. Since perfectly ripe tomatoes aren't always available, we turned to trusty (and prep-free) canned tomatoes. As for the technique, we tested to determine whether we could simply throw the aromatics into the blender without blooming them first to build flavor. We found that microwaving the onion with butter, tomato paste, and salt really deepened the flavor of the soup and was worth the quick extra step. Brown sugar was key to mellowing the acidity from the tomatoes. For richness, we added heavy cream 1 minute before the soup was fully pureed. Serve with Classic Croutons, if desired.

1. Microwave onion, tomato paste, butter, and salt in bowl, stirring occasionally, until onion is softened, about 5 minutes; transfer to Ace blender along with tomatoes and their juice, broth, and sugar. Lock lid in place, then select soup program 2 (for creamy soups).

2. Pause program 1 minute before it has completed. Carefully remove lid and add cream. Return lid and resume program. Adjust consistency with extra broth as needed and season with salt and pepper to taste. Sprinkle individual portions with chives before serving.

CLASSIC CROUTONS
MAKES ABOUT 1 CUP

1 tablespoon unsalted butter
2 slices hearty white sandwich bread,
   cut into ½-inch pieces
½ teaspoon minced fresh thyme (optional)

Melt butter in 10-inch skillet over medium heat. Add bread and thyme, if using, and cook, stirring frequently, until light golden brown, 3 to 5 minutes. Season with salt and pepper to taste.

SPICED CROUTONS
Add ¼ teaspoon paprika, ⅛ teaspoon cumin, and pinch cayenne to skillet with melted butter and cook until fragrant, about 30 seconds; proceed with recipe as directed.

CARROT-GINGER SOUP

SERVES 2 TO 4

TOTAL TIME
1 hour

1½ **pounds carrots, peeled and cut into 1½-inch pieces**

3 **cups chicken or vegetable broth, plus extra as needed**

1 **small onion, cut into 1-inch pieces**

1 **tablespoon unsalted butter**

1 **(1-inch) piece fresh ginger, peeled and quartered**

1 **garlic clove, peeled**

1 **teaspoon minced fresh thyme or ¼ teaspoon dried**

1 **teaspoon table salt**

1 **teaspoon sugar**

¼ **cup minced fresh chives**

WHY THIS RECIPE WORKS Sometimes the simplest recipes get overcomplicated as more and more versions appear. Case in point: carrot-ginger soup, whose flavors often get elbowed out with the addition of other vegetables, fruits, or dairy. But this simple, creamy, pared-down version is velvety smooth with clean carrot flavor and subtle ginger background notes. Plus, making this soup could not be easier: just throw everything into the blender except for the garnishes and start the soup program for creamy soups. For richness we added just a tablespoon of butter while a small amount of sugar enhances the natural sweetness of the carrots. Onion, garlic, and thyme added just the right savory element. We finished with a simple garnish of chopped chives to provide texture and tang. Serve with Classic Croutons (page 23) and a drizzle of yogurt, if desired.

1. Add carrots, broth, onion, butter, ginger, garlic, thyme, salt, and sugar to Ace blender. Lock lid in place, then select soup program 2 (for creamy soups).

2. Once program has completed, carefully remove lid. Adjust soup consistency with extra broth as needed and season with salt and pepper to taste. Sprinkle individual portions with chives before serving.

BUTTERNUT SQUASH SOUP

SERVES 2 TO 4

TOTAL TIME
1 hour

1½ **pounds peeled and
    seeded butternut squash,
    cut into 1½-inch pieces**

2 **cups chicken or vegetable
   broth, plus extra as
   needed**

1 **large shallot, chopped**

2 **tablespoons unsalted
   butter**

1½ **teaspoons honey**

¾ **teaspoon table salt**

WHY THIS RECIPE WORKS This simple, velvety-smooth butternut squash soup comes together easily using the blender. And it is super easy to make too—there is no need to microwave the chopped shallot or bloom any spices first due to its long cooking time in the blender. Because there is so much butternut squash (and fairly large pieces, at that), during the first half of cooking the squash doesn't move around much during the brief periods of pulsing. Don't worry, your machine isn't stuck or broken; as the squash cooks and breaks down, the mixture does start to move around. Plenty of squash and not much liquid also mean that the soup stays relatively thick, without the need for cream, which would have masked the nuanced flavors. We developed a deeply flavorful variation with a Southwestern profile using canned chipotles and cumin. Serve with Spiced Croutons (page 23) and a dollop of sour cream, if desired.

1. Add all ingredients to Ace blender. Lock lid in place, then select soup program 2 (for creamy soups).

2. Once program has completed, carefully remove lid. Adjust soup consistency with extra broth as needed and season with salt and pepper to taste. Serve.

SOUTHWESTERN BUTTERNUT SQUASH SOUP
Add 1 teaspoon minced canned chipotle chile in adobo sauce and ½ teaspoon cumin to blender with squash. Sprinkle individual portions with 1 tablespoon chopped fresh cilantro before serving.

SUPER GREENS SOUP

SERVES 2 TO 4

TOTAL TIME
45 minutes

3½ cups chicken or vegetable broth, plus extra as needed

1 small onion, cut into ¾-inch pieces

⅓ cup Arborio rice

2 tablespoons extra-virgin olive oil

3 garlic cloves, peeled

¾ teaspoon table salt, divided

¼ cup whole-milk yogurt

1 teaspoon minced fresh tarragon or parsley

¼ teaspoon finely grated lemon zest plus ½ teaspoon juice

6 ounces Swiss chard, stemmed and chopped

4 ounces kale, stemmed and chopped

1 cup baby arugula

WHY THIS RECIPE WORKS This deceptively delicious, silky-smooth soup delivers a big dose of healthy greens, boasts a deep complex flavor, and leaves you feeling virtuous but fully satisfied. As a bonus, the creamy soup function makes it a snap to make: We added all the ingredients for the soup except the greens to the blender at once, no microwaving required. For the greens we chose a mix of Swiss chard, kale, and peppery arugula. Instead of precooking them, we added them to the blender after 12 minutes of the cycle with the other ingredients, reserving the more delicate arugula to add for the final minute. Many recipes we found used potatoes as a thickener for this soup, but they lent an overwhelmingly earthy flavor. Instead, we tried using Arborio rice. The rice's high starch content thickened the soup to a velvety, lush consistency without clouding its bright, vegetal flavors, and we added it in the beginning with the broth and aromatics. For a vibrant finish, we whisked together whole milk yogurt, minced tarragon, and lemon zest and juice and drizzled it over the top. This is a soup that is sure to impress as it is stunningly beautiful with layers of complex earthy flavor.

1. Add broth, onion, rice, oil, garlic, and ½ teaspoon salt to Ace blender. Lock lid in place, then select soup program 2 (for creamy soups).

2. Meanwhile, combine yogurt, tarragon, lemon zest and juice, and remaining ¼ teaspoon salt in bowl; refrigerate until ready to serve.

3. Pause program 12 minutes before it has completed. Carefully remove lid and stir in chard and kale until completely submerged. Return lid and resume program. Pause program 1 minute before it has completed. Stir in arugula. Return lid and resume program. Once program has completed, adjust soup consistency with extra broth as needed and season with salt and pepper to taste. Drizzle individual portions with yogurt sauce before serving.

CORN CHOWDER

SERVES 2 TO 4

TOTAL TIME
50 minutes

3 cups frozen corn, thawed

2½ cups chicken broth

3 ounces andouille sausage, cut into ½-inch pieces

1 small onion, cut into ¾-inch pieces

1 red potato, unpeeled, cut into ½-inch pieces

¼ cup heavy cream

2 garlic cloves, minced

½ teaspoon minced fresh thyme or ⅛ teaspoon dried

¼ teaspoon table salt

¼ teaspoon pepper

2 tablespoons minced fresh parsley

WHY THIS RECIPE WORKS What's the secret to easy corn chowder loaded with fresh-from-the-cob flavor? Skip the cob and go straight to the freezer section! Frozen corn is processed at the peak of the season; ensuring its flavor is bright and fresh any time of year. Chopped andouille sausage contributed a smoky backbone to this hearty and appealing blender soup. Some chicken broth improved the flavor of our chowder, while a small amount of heavy cream provided just enough richness. A red potato, garlic, and onion added substance and the right aromatic notes, and a sprinkling of fresh parsley was the perfect finishing touch. Using thawed frozen corn cuts down on the preheat time by 4 minutes. Blending the chowder just briefly after cooking releases some starch from the corn, and breaks down some of the kernels to thicken the chowder perfectly. We prefer the smoky flavor and spice of andouille sausage here, but kielbasa sausage can be substituted.

1. Add corn, broth, sausage, onion, potato, cream, garlic, thyme, salt, and pepper to Ace blender. Lock lid in place, then select soup program 1 (for chunky soups).

2. Once program has completed, process soup on medium speed until slightly thickened but still chunky, about 2 seconds. Carefully remove lid, stir in parsley, and season with salt and pepper to taste. Serve.

LOADED BAKED POTATO SOUP

SERVES 2 TO 4

TOTAL TIME
1 hour

4 slices bacon

1½ pounds russet potatoes,
   peeled and cut into
   ¾-inch pieces

2½ cups chicken broth,
   plus extra as needed

1 small onion, cut into
   ¾-inch pieces

¼ cup heavy cream

2 garlic cloves, minced

½ teaspoon minced fresh
   thyme or ⅛ teaspoon
   dried

4 ounces sharp cheddar
   cheese, shredded (1 cup),
   plus extra for serving

¼ cup sour cream

2 scallions, sliced thin

WHY THIS RECIPE WORKS Baking your potatoes for baked potato soup can take up to an hour—and then you still have to make the soup. So, for a baked potato soup that truly tasted like baked potatoes but didn't involve actually baking them, we simply cut them into chunks and added them to the blender along with broth, cream, a little onion, and fresh thyme. For the classic smoky bacon flavor that is the hallmark of this soup, we microwaved bacon and chopped it, adding some to the blender and reserving the rest for serving. For richness, once the soup was fully processed and heated in the blender, we simply added a modest amount of sharp cheddar and sour cream, letting it dissolve into the soup until it turned velvety smooth and rich. This loaded baked potato soup is comfort food at its best.

1. Line large plate with double layer of coffee filters. Arrange bacon in even layer on prepared plate and microwave until crisp, about 5 minutes. Let bacon cool slightly, then chop fine. Set aside half of bacon for serving.

2. Add remaining bacon, potatoes, broth, onion, cream, garlic, and thyme to Ace blender. Lock lid in place, then select soup program 1 (for chunky soups).

3. Once program has completed, carefully remove lid and stir in cheddar and sour cream until cheese is melted and fully combined. Adjust consistency of soup with extra broth as needed and season with salt and pepper to taste. Sprinkle individual portions with reserved bacon, scallions, and extra cheddar before serving.

BLACK BEAN SOUP

SERVES 2 TO 4

TOTAL TIME
1 hour

- 2 (15-ounce) cans black beans, rinsed

- 2 cups chicken or vegetable broth

- 1 red bell pepper, stemmed, seeded, and cut into ½-inch pieces

- 1 small onion, cut into ½-inch pieces

- 3 garlic cloves, minced

- ¼ ounce dried porcini mushrooms, rinsed and chopped

- 1 tablespoon extra-virgin olive oil

- 1½ teaspoons minced fresh oregano or ½ teaspoon dried

- ½ teaspoon ground cumin

- ½ teaspoon chili powder

- ¼ teaspoon table salt

- ¼ cup minced fresh cilantro

WHY THIS RECIPE WORKS This black bean soup is super easy to make given that it relies on canned beans, and since it has plenty of spices and aromatics, it has a great balance of sweet and spicy flavors. We found that there was no need to microwave the aromatics in advance here, which also kept the process simpler. We cut the onion and sweet red bell pepper into chunks and let the blender do the rest of the work. The chunky soup function worked perfectly for this soup. One secret to the backbone of flavor in this soup is dried porcini mushrooms, which we rinsed and minced and added to the blender with the aromatics and spices—their umami punch adds a depth of flavor that is surprising. For just the right texture, after the chunky soup program was finished, we processed the soup for a few seconds to break down some of the beans. Serve with sour cream and lime wedges.

1. Add beans, broth, bell pepper, onion, garlic, mushrooms, oil, oregano, cumin, chili powder, and salt in Ace blender. Lock lid in place, then select soup program 1 (for chunky soups).

2. Once program has completed, process soup on medium speed until slightly thickened but still chunky, about 3 seconds. Carefully remove lid, stir in cilantro, and season with salt and pepper to taste. Serve.

HEARTY WHITE BEAN SOUP WITH SAUSAGE AND CABBAGE

SERVES 2 TO 4

TOTAL TIME
1 hour

1 (15-ounce) can cannellini beans, rinsed

2½ cups chicken broth

1 small onion, cut into ¾-inch pieces

1 carrot, peeled and cut into ¾-inch pieces

1 celery rib, cut into ¾-inch pieces

4 ounces kielbasa sausage, cut into ½-inch pieces

2 garlic cloves, minced

1 tablespoon tomato paste

1 tablespoon extra-virgin olive oil

½ teaspoon minced fresh oregano or ⅛ teaspoon dried

¼ teaspoon table salt

¼ head savoy cabbage, cored and cut into 1-inch pieces (1½ cups)

WHY THIS RECIPE WORKS With few ingredients to distract from flaws like mushy beans or a thin broth, white bean soup is rarely well prepared, so making it in a blender seemed like a high bar. But to our surprise it was easy to make (everything could be added to the blender at once) and delicious. To create a richly perfumed base for our blender soup, we selected the ingredients carefully since we would not be starting by cooking the sausage. A classic mirepoix (onion, carrot, and celery) was a given, and tomato paste added the depth of flavor we missed from browning the sausage. Chopped kielbasa ensured this soup had a flavorful kick. We added canned beans straight to the blender, where the gentle simmering heat helped them cook through evenly. The cabbage was perfectly tender by the end of cooking yet retained its appealing frilly texture. Serve with crusty bread to dip into the broth.

Add all ingredients to Ace blender. Lock lid in place, then select soup program 1 (for chunky soups). Once program has completed, carefully remove lid and season with salt and pepper to taste. Serve.

RED LENTIL SOUP WITH NORTH AFRICAN SPICES

SERVES 2 TO 4

TOTAL TIME
50 minutes

- 1 **small onion, cut into ½-inch pieces**
- 1 **tablespoon extra-virgin olive oil**
- 1 **tablespoon tomato paste**
- ½ **teaspoon ground coriander**
- ¼ **teaspoon ground cumin**
- ⅛ **teaspoon ground ginger**
- ¼ **teaspoon table salt**
- ¼ **teaspoon pepper**
- 4 **cups vegetable or chicken broth, plus extra as needed**
- 1¼ **cups red lentils, picked over and rinsed**
- 1 **tablespoon lemon juice, plus extra for seasoning**
- 2 **tablespoons harissa**
- ¼ **cup chopped fresh cilantro**

WHY THIS RECIPE WORKS Small red lentils are one of our favorite legumes; they break down quickly into a creamy, thick puree when cooked—perfect for a satisfying soup. Their mild flavor does require a bit of embellishment, so we quickly bloomed coriander, cumin, and ginger along with olive oil, tomato paste, and a chopped onion before adding them to the blender with broth and the lentils. A generous dose of lemon juice at the end brought the flavors into focus and a sprinkle of fresh cilantro completed the transformation of common-place ingredients into an exotic yet comforting soup. Do not substitute other varieties of lentils for the red lentils here; red lentils produce a very different texture. Harissa is a traditional North African condiment that is great for serving with a variety of soups, salads, and proteins. You can find harissa in the international aisle of most well-stocked supermarkets; if not, extra-virgin olive oil will work well.

1. Microwave onion, oil, tomato paste, coriander, cumin, ginger, salt, and pepper in bowl, stirring occasionally, until onion is softened, about 5 minutes; transfer to Ace blender along with broth and lentils. Lock lid in place, then select soup program 1 (for chunky soups).

2. Once program has completed, carefully remove lid and adjust consistency with extra broth as needed. Stir in lemon juice and season with salt and extra lemon juice to taste. Drizzle individual portions with harissa and sprinkle with cilantro before serving.

EASY MAINS AND SIDES YOU'RE SURE TO ACE

CHICKEN CACCIATORE

SERVES 4

TOTAL TIME
50 minutes

8 ounces cremini mushrooms, trimmed and quartered

1 small onion, cut into ¾-inch pieces

1 teaspoon extra-virgin olive oil

1 (15-ounce) can crushed tomatoes

1 cup chicken broth

½ cup jarred roasted red peppers, cut into ½-inch-thick strips

¼ ounce dried porcini mushrooms, rinsed and chopped

2 garlic cloves, minced

1 teaspoon minced fresh oregano or ¼ teaspoon dried

1 teaspoon table salt

¼ teaspoon red pepper flakes

2 cups coarsely shredded cooked chicken

2 tablespoons chopped fresh parsley

Grated Parmesan cheese

WHY THIS RECIPE WORKS Chicken cacciatore is a classic Italian dish known for its "hunter style" ingredients like mushrooms, chicken, garlic, and fresh herbs. It's this combination of flavors that make it so rich and hearty, the kind of comfort food you find in Italy. Since it usually uses bone-in chicken parts and requires both stovetop browning and a long braising time, it seemed a bit of a stretch to assemble it in a blender, but building a flavorful cacciatore sauce proved to be easy. We chose to use earthy cremini mushrooms, and to soften them we decided to microwave them with chopped onion and extra-virgin olive oil. Crushed tomatoes, which have a lot of body without the need for reduction, formed the base of the sauce to which we added convenient jarred roasted red peppers, dried porcini mushrooms (for added depth of flavor), garlic, oregano, and red pepper flakes. The chunky soup function of the blender worked its magic on this combination of ingredients, turning out a thick and robust sauce to which we simply added tender chunks of cooked chicken and a shower of chopped parsley. We prefer to shred the chicken into large 2-inch pieces here. Serve over polenta, egg noodles, or rice.

1. Microwave cremini mushrooms, onion, and oil in bowl, stirring occasionally, until vegetables are softened, about 5 minutes. Drain vegetables and transfer to Ace blender along with tomatoes, broth, red peppers, porcini mushrooms, garlic, oregano, salt, and pepper flakes. Lock lid in place, then select soup program 1 (for chunky soups).

2. Pause program 2 minutes before it has completed. Carefully remove lid and stir in chicken. Return lid and replace lid cap with food tamper. Resume program, using tamper as needed to stir ingredients. Once program has completed, stir in parsley and season with salt and pepper to taste. Sprinkle individual portions with Parmesan cheese before serving.

CHICKEN TAGINE WITH CHICKPEAS AND APRICOTS

SERVES 4

TOTAL TIME
1 hour

1 small onion, cut into ¾-inch pieces

1 tablespoon extra-virgin olive oil

¾ teaspoon table salt

½ teaspoon ground cumin

¼ teaspoon ground cinnamon

¼ teaspoon ground coriander

3 garlic cloves, minced

2 cups chicken broth

1 (15-ounce) can chickpeas, rinsed

½ cup dried apricots, halved

1 carrot, peeled, halved lengthwise, and sliced ¾-inch thick

½ teaspoon grated lemon zest plus 1 tablespoon juice

1½ cups coarsely shredded cooked chicken

2 tablespoons chopped fresh cilantro

WHY THIS RECIPE WORKS Tagines are a North African specialty: exotically spiced, assertively flavored stews slow-cooked in earthenware vessels of the same name. Traditional recipes usually require a time-consuming cooking method, a special pot (the tagine), and hard-to-find ingredients. Over the years in the test kitchen we have developed many recipes to simplify the making of tagines, but this blender rendition is the fastest, putting a great chicken tagine on the weeknight dinner rotation. After microwaving the spices and chopped onion, we added everything with the exception of shredded cooked chicken, cilantro, and lemon juice to the blender. Sweet chopped carrots, a hefty amount of dried apricots, and a can of chickpeas went into the blender along with chicken broth and lemon zest. As they cooked, the apricots broke down a bit, adding both texture and sweet flavor to the sauce. As for the chicken, we simply stopped the blender a couple of minutes before the cycle was over and added it to allow it to heat through perfectly. Additional lemon juice before serving balanced out the sweet flavors and grassy cilantro added brightness. We prefer to shred the chicken into large 2-inch pieces here. Serve over couscous or rice.

1. Microwave onion, oil, salt, cumin, cinnamon, coriander, and garlic in bowl, stirring occasionally, until onion is softened, about 5 minutes. Transfer to Ace blender along with broth, chickpeas, apricots, carrot, and lemon zest. Lock lid in place, then select soup program 1 (for chunky soups).

2. Pause program 2 minutes before it has completed. Carefully remove lid and stir in chicken. Return lid and replace lid cap with food tamper. Resume program, using tamper as needed to stir ingredients. Once program has completed, stir in cilantro and lemon juice and season with salt and pepper to taste. Serve.

MOLE CHICKEN TACOS

SERVES 4

TOTAL TIME
1 hour

1 red onion (½ cut
   into ¾-inch pieces,
   ½ chopped fine)

2 dried ancho chiles,
   stemmed, seeded,
   and torn into ½-inch
   pieces (½ cup)

1 tablespoon vegetable oil

1 tablespoon sesame seeds

1 tablespoon unsweetened
   cocoa powder

2 garlic cloves, peeled

¼ teaspoon ground
   cinnamon

½ teaspoon table salt

2 cups chicken broth

¾ cup canned diced
   tomatoes, drained

¼ cup raisins

2 tablespoons dry-roasted
   unsalted peanuts

4 cups shredded cooked
   chicken

12 (6-inch) corn tortillas,
   warmed

1 cup fresh cilantro leaves

   Lime wedges

WHY THIS RECIPE WORKS Since making the quintessential Mexican sauce known as mole involves the blender anyway, we set out to use the Ace blender to create a plush sauce and put mole chicken tacos on the dinner table in record speed. First, we bypassed the usual step of toasting chiles and softening aromatics in a skillet and turned to the microwave instead. And while a traditional mole can be an involved affair using multiple types of chiles, nuts, seeds, and chocolate, we were able to re-create its hallmark rich flavor with just pantry ingredients: dried ancho chiles, onion, garlic, sesame seeds, and dry-roasted peanuts. A little cocoa powder and raisins plus cinnamon added richness and depth with the right touch of sweetness. Chicken broth and canned diced tomatoes gave our sauce its body and just the right texture. The creamy soup function on the blender delivered a luxurious and piping hot mole, and the shredded chicken warmed through in just minutes.

1. Microwave onion pieces (reserve finely chopped onion), anchos, oil, sesame seeds, cocoa, garlic, cinnamon, and salt in bowl, stirring occasionally, until onion is softened, about 5 minutes. Transfer to Ace blender along with broth, tomatoes, raisins, and peanuts. Lock lid in place, then select soup program 2 (for creamy soups).

2. Once program has completed, carefully remove lid and stir in chicken. Let sit until heated through, about 2 minutes. Season with salt and pepper to taste. Serve filling on tortillas, topped with cilantro and finely chopped onion, passing lime wedges separately.

EASY GROUND BEEF CHILI

SERVES 4

TOTAL TIME
40 minutes

1 small onion, cut into ¾-inch pieces

2 tablespoons chili powder

5 garlic cloves, peeled

1 tablespoon vegetable oil

1 tablespoon tomato paste

2 teaspoons ground cumin

1½ teaspoons dried oregano

¾ teaspoon table salt

¼ teaspoon pepper

1 (28-ounce) can whole peeled tomatoes

½ cup chicken broth

12 ounces 90 percent lean ground beef

1 (15-ounce) can kidney beans, rinsed

WHY THIS RECIPE WORKS A great beef chili usually starts with developing layers of flavor by sautéing aromatics and spices, then the beef, then adding the other ingredients, usually in a large Dutch oven. It involves lots of chopping and lots of standing by the stove. For a weeknight-friendly chili we could make in the Ace blender, we decided to create the tomatoey chili base first, using the blender to assemble a thick, flavorful mixture. But first we bloomed the spices in the microwave along with whole peeled garlic cloves, chunks of onion, and tomato paste. We added this mixture to the blender along with a large can of whole tomatoes and processed it until nearly smooth. This thick mixture provided a base for our chili minus any simmering or reduction. To this base we added canned kidney beans and selected the chunky soup function on the blender. And what about the ground beef? We broke it into smallish chunks, paused the soup function, and added the beef 15 minutes before the function ended. The beef cooked through perfectly in the hot chili base and all the flavors and textures melded into a fragrant chili—no stovetop work required. Serve with your favorite chili toppings.

1. Microwave onion, chili powder, garlic, oil, tomato paste, cumin, oregano, salt, and pepper in bowl, stirring occasionally, until onion is softened, about 5 minutes. Transfer to Ace blender along with tomatoes and their juice and broth. Lock lid in place, then process on medium speed until vegetables are finely ground, about 30 seconds. Scrape down sides of blender jar. Return lid and process on high speed until smooth, about 1 minute.

2. Select soup program 1 (for chunky soups). Meanwhile, break ground beef into rough ½-inch pieces; transfer to plate and refrigerate until ready to use.

3. Pause program 15 minutes before it has completed. Carefully remove lid and stir beans and ground beef pieces into chili until completely submerged. Return lid and resume program, pausing occasionally to stir ingredients that have settled to base of blender jar. Once program has completed, season with salt and pepper to taste. Serve.

SWEET AND SOUR BEEF WITH SHIITAKES AND BELL PEPPER

SERVES 4

TOTAL TIME
50 minutes

¾ **cup pineapple juice, divided**

2 **tablespoons packed light brown sugar**

2 **tablespoons soy sauce, plus extra for seasoning**

2 **tablespoons ketchup**

2 **tablespoons rice vinegar**

2 **teaspoons grated fresh ginger**

1 **garlic clove, minced**

½ **teaspoon Asian chili-garlic sauce**

6 **ounces shiitake mushrooms, stemmed and sliced ¼-inch thick**

1 **red bell pepper, stemmed, seeded, and cut into ¼-inch-wide strips**

1 **teaspoon vegetable oil**

1½ **tablespoons cornstarch**

1 **pound top sirloin steak, trimmed**

2 **scallions, sliced thin on bias**

WHY THIS RECIPE WORKS Imagine making a beef stir-fry with a sweet and sour sauce without even using a skillet. Here the blender does all the work with a little assist from the microwave to soften the vegetables. So, first we added the sauce ingredients to the blender, a combination of pineapple juice, brown sugar, and ketchup for sweetness, and rice vinegar, ginger, garlic, and Asian chili-garlic sauce for the balancing Asian flavors and punch. To heat and blend this mixture we chose the chunky soup function, stopping it 10 minutes before the cycle had completed so we could add thinly sliced sirloin steak and the microwaved vegetables. Given the bulk of the steak and vegetables we found it necessary to pause the function a few times to give the mixture a stir so the steak could cook through. And we also paused it toward the end to add a thickening slurry made with cornstarch and a little extra pineapple juice. Once done, we were left with a complex sauce and an appealing ratio of delicious steak to perfectly cooked vegetables, ready to serve over rice for a complete meal. No one will ever guess this Chinese classic was made so easily and successfully in a blender. To make the steak easier to slice thin, freeze it for 15 minutes.

1. Add ½ cup pineapple juice, sugar, soy sauce, ketchup, vinegar, ginger, garlic, and chili-garlic sauce to Ace blender. Lock lid in place, then select soup program 1 (for chunky soups). Meanwhile, microwave mushrooms, bell pepper, and oil in bowl, stirring occasionally, until vegetables are softened, about 5 minutes; drain and set aside. In separate bowl, whisk remaining ¼ cup pineapple juice and cornstarch together; set aside.

2. Slice steak ⅛-inch thick against grain on bias, then cut slices into rough 2-inch pieces. Pause program 10 minutes before it has completed. Carefully remove lid and stir in steak and vegetables. Return lid and replace lid cap with food tamper. Resume program, using tamper as needed to stir ingredients.

3. Pause program 2 minutes before it has completed. Stir in cornstarch mixture, return lid, and resume program. Once program has completed, season with extra soy sauce to taste. Sprinkle individual portions with scallions before serving.

BARBECUED PORK SANDWICHES

SERVES 4

TOTAL TIME
35 minutes

½ **cup ketchup**

¼ **cup chicken broth**

½ **small onion, chopped fine**

3 **tablespoons plus
1 teaspoon molasses,
divided**

3 **tablespoons cider vinegar,
divided**

1 **tablespoon
Worcestershire sauce**

4 **teaspoons Dijon mustard,
divided**

1 **garlic clove, minced**

½ **teaspoon chili powder**

¼ **teaspoon liquid smoke**

1 **pound pork tenderloin,
trimmed**

2 **tablespoons mayonnaise**

2 **cups shredded
coleslaw mix**

4 **hamburger buns**

WHY THIS RECIPE WORKS Making barbecued or pulled pork for sandwiches is usually a bit of a production and involves the long, slow cooking of a marbled pork butt roast nestled in a fragrant sauce. So how could we possibly translate that recipe to a blender? Well, we decided to make a classic barbecue sauce using the chunky soup function and we imagined all the ingredients would meld together while the blender whirred and the sauce came up to temperature. Then we would poach very thinly sliced pieces of pork tenderloin right in the sauce. We were aiming for a tangy ketchup-based sauce, so we added all the necessary ingredients along with a little broth (to prevent the sauce from burning given the sugar in the ketchup and molasses). Liquid smoke gave our sauce the requisite smoky flavor in short order. While the sauce was cooking in the blender we had time to make a quick coleslaw using convenient bagged coleslaw mix and also to halve and thinly slice the pork. We stopped the sauce 10 minutes before the cooking cycle was finished and added the pork, which cooked through perfectly and absorbed the flavor of the tangy sauce. Tender pork piled high on a bun topped with crisp coleslaw, this blender-made sandwich is a winner. You can find shredded coleslaw mix in the packaged salad aisle at the grocery store. To make the pork tenderloin easier to slice thin, freeze it for 15 minutes.

1. Add ketchup, broth, onion, 3 tablespoons molasses, 2 tablespoons vinegar, Worcestershire, 1 tablespoon mustard, garlic, chili powder, and liquid smoke to Ace blender. Lock lid in place, then select soup program 1 (for chunky soups).

2. Meanwhile, halve tenderloin lengthwise, then slice crosswise ⅛-inch thick; transfer to plate and refrigerate until ready to use. Whisk remaining 1 teaspoon molasses, remaining 1 tablespoon vinegar, remaining 1 teaspoon mustard, and mayonnaise together in medium bowl. Add coleslaw mix and toss to coat. Season with salt and pepper to taste; refrigerate until ready to serve.

3. Pause program 10 minutes before it has completed. Carefully remove lid and stir pork pieces into sauce until completely submerged. Return lid and replace lid cap with food tamper. Resume program, using tamper as needed to stir ingredients. Once program has completed, season with salt and pepper to taste. Serve pork on buns, topped with coleslaw.

THAI SHRIMP CURRY

SERVES 4

TOTAL TIME
40 minutes

1 (14-ounce) can coconut milk

3 Thai chiles, stemmed, seeded, and chopped

¼ cup fresh cilantro leaves

6 garlic cloves, peeled and smashed

1 lemon grass stalk, trimmed to bottom 6 inches and chopped

1 (2-inch) piece ginger, peeled and chopped

1 tablespoon fish sauce

2 teaspoons packed brown sugar

1 teaspoon grated lime zest, plus lime wedges for serving

1 teaspoon ground cumin

6 ounces sugar snap peas, strings removed

1 red bell pepper, stemmed, seeded, and cut into ½-inch pieces

1 teaspoon vegetable oil

1 pound extra-large shrimp (21 to 25 per pound), peeled, deveined, and tails removed

¼ cup fresh Thai basil leaves

Lime wedges

WHY THIS RECIPE WORKS Unlike Indian curries, Thai curries almost always contain coconut milk. Also, they tilt the spice balance towards fresh aromatics in the form of a homemade chile paste. For a streamlined Thai shrimp curry dish that was scaled down in effort but not in flavor, we eliminated homemade curry paste and went with a simplified sauce that could be easily assembled in the blender. A little chicken broth cut through the richness of a full can of coconut milk, while easy-to-find Thai staples such as Thai chiles (serrano or jalapeño chiles make great substitutes), fish sauce, lemon grass, brown sugar, lime juice, cilantro, and basil offered welcome complexity. Quick-cooking shrimp, snap peas, and red bell pepper paired well with our flavorful sauce. For a smooth sauce we found we needed to blend the ingredients first before heating it up in the blender. The vegetables needed a quick spin in the microwave to ensure tenderness and we also drained off excess liquid so as not to dilute our delicious curry sauce. We added the vegetables and the shrimp to the blender partway through the cook cycle. Note that because of the volume in the blender, the temperature of the sauce drops dramatically when you add the vegetables and shrimp—the shrimp effectively poaches at a low gentle temperature until just cooked and tender, while the snap peas and bell pepper remain tender-crisp. If you can't find Thai basil leaves, regular basil will work fine. Serve over rice.

1. Place coconut milk, chiles, cilantro, garlic, lemon grass, ginger, fish sauce, sugar, lime zest, and cumin in Ace blender. Lock lid in place, then process on high speed until smooth, about 2 minutes. Scrape down sides of blender jar. Return lid and select soup program 1 (for chunky soups).

2. Meanwhile, microwave snap peas, bell pepper, and oil in bowl until vegetables are just beginning to soften, about 3 minutes; drain and set aside.

3. Pause program 12 minutes before it has completed. Carefully remove lid and stir snap peas, bell pepper, and shrimp into sauce until fully submerged. Return lid and replace lid cap with food tamper. Resume program, using tamper as needed to stir ingredients. Once program has completed, stir in basil and season with salt to taste. Serve with lime wedges.

INDIAN VEGETABLE CURRY

SERVES 4

TOTAL TIME
1 hour

8 ounces cauliflower florets,
cut into 2-inch pieces

1 red potato, unpeeled,
cut into ¾-inch pieces

1 small onion, chopped

3 garlic cloves, minced

1 tablespoon grated
fresh ginger

1 tablespoon tomato paste

1 tablespoon vegetable oil

4 teaspoons curry powder

¾ teaspoon table salt

2½ cups chicken or vegetable
broth, plus extra as
needed

1 (15-ounce) can chickpeas,
rinsed

¾ cup frozen peas, thawed

¼ cup chopped fresh
cilantro

WHY THIS RECIPE WORKS Curries usually require a laundry list of spices and hours of simmering time, but we wanted to create a deeply flavorful Indian-inspired curry sauce quickly in the blender. And we wanted to add enough vegetables to make a satisfying meal. To give our sauce a nice backbone, a hefty amount of curry powder along with onion, garlic, fresh ginger, and tomato paste was all we needed. For the vegetables, cauliflower, potato, peas, and convenient canned chickpeas made for a classic combination easy to incorporate into our blender sauce. But we found that we needed to give the sturdy chunks of potato and the fibrous cauliflower florets a head start if they were to cook through fully in the blender sauce, so we microwaved them along with the aromatics just to soften them a bit. The chunky soup function proved to be our best option because it cooked the vegetables without breaking them down too much; we added them along with the aromatics, chickpeas, and broth, stopping the cycle just a few minutes early to add the peas. The chickpeas broke down a bit as did the cauliflower, both of which helped thicken our now fragrant sauce. Serve over rice.

1. Microwave cauliflower, potato, onion, garlic, ginger, tomato paste, oil, curry powder, and salt in bowl, stirring occasionally, until cauliflower and potato begin to soften, about 5 minutes; transfer to Ace blender along with broth and chickpeas. Lock lid in place, then select soup program 1 (for chunky soups), pausing occasionally to redistribute ingredients by hand.

2. Pause program 3 minutes before it has completed. Carefully remove lid and add peas. Return lid and resume program. Once program has completed, season with salt and pepper to taste. Sprinkle individual portions with cilantro before serving.

ZOODLES PUTTANESCA

SERVES 2

TOTAL TIME
40 minutes

½ small onion, cut into ¾-inch pieces

1 tablespoon extra-virgin olive oil

1 tablespoon tomato paste

1 garlic clove, peeled

¼ teaspoon red pepper flakes

1 (14.5-ounce) can whole peeled tomatoes

2 tablespoons coarsely chopped kalamata olives

1 tablespoon capers, rinsed

2 tablespoons minced fresh parsley

12 ounces zucchini noodles

2 tablespoons toasted pine nuts

Grated Parmesan cheese

WHY THIS RECIPE WORKS Spiralized noodles are all the rage because they offer a healthy but flavorful alternative to carb-loaded pasta and starchy sides. Plus, if you don't want to spiralize your own noodles, they are readily available to buy already cut, making a dish like this a snap to make. Here we wanted to combine zucchini noodles, aka zoodles, with a puttanesca-like marinara sauce that boasted a punch from red pepper flakes and briny flavor from capers and olives. To create our sauce we simply microwaved the aromatics along with tomato paste and some oil then added them along with the tomatoes and their juice to the blender and selected the chunky soup function. When that cycle was over we switched over to the blender mode to create a sauce with just the right body and consistency. Next we simply added the olives, capers, and the zoodles, letting them soften for just a few minutes. Toasted pine nuts added welcome crunch and flavor to our easy blender zoodles puttanesca. You can find zucchini noodles in the prepared vegetables section of most well-stocked supermarkets.

1. Microwave onion, oil, tomato paste, garlic, and pepper flakes in bowl, stirring occasionally, until onion is softened, about 3 minutes; transfer to Ace blender along with tomatoes and their juice. Lock lid in place, then select soup program 1 (for chunky soups).

2. Once program has completed, process sauce on medium speed until slightly thickened but still chunky, about 5 seconds. Carefully remove lid and stir in olives, capers, parsley, and zucchini noodles. Return lid and let sit until noodles are tender, about 5 minutes. Season with salt to taste. Sprinkle individual portions with pine nuts and Parmesan before serving.

CREAMY MASHED CAULIFLOWER

SERVES 2 TO 4

TOTAL TIME
25 minutes

1 head cauliflower
(1½ pounds), cored and
cut into 1-inch florets

¼ cup water

1 tablespoon unsalted
butter

½ teaspoon table salt

WHY THIS RECIPE WORKS Mashed cauliflower makes a great, healthier alternative to mashed potatoes and because of its low insoluble fiber, it doesn't require cream to turn it velvety smooth. Since the blender is the perfect appliance for rendering cooked cauliflower smooth and creamy, we wondered whether the Ace blender could both cook and blend it with one simple touch of a button. Unfortunately, when we added enough water to process the cauliflower, it turned into a soup rather than a mash. But the simple step of microwaving the florets with water, salt, and butter solved the problem; we then could use the hot puree program to finish the task. We love that it's easy to add flavorings to this simple mash.

Microwave all ingredients in covered bowl, stirring occasionally, until cauliflower is softened, about 8 minutes; transfer to Ace blender. Lock lid in place, then select puree program 2 (for hard vegetables). Once program has completed, carefully remove lid and season with salt and pepper to taste. Serve.

CREAMY MASHED CAULIFLOWER WITH LEMON AND HERBS
Add ½ teaspoon minced fresh thyme to bowl with remaining ingredients. Stir ½ teaspoon grated lemon zest and 2 tablespoons chopped fresh parsley or basil into cauliflower before seasoning

CREAMY MASHED CAULIFLOWER WITH ROASTED GARLIC AND PARMESAN
You can find roasted garlic at the salad bar or in the prepared vegetables section of most well-stocked supermarkets.

Substitute extra-virgin olive oil for butter and add 4 cloves roasted garlic to blender with ingredients. Stir ½ cup grated Parmesan cheese into cauliflower before seasoning.

BUTTERNUT SQUASH PUREE

SERVES 2 TO 4

TOTAL TIME
25 minutes

- 1½ **pounds peeled butternut squash, cut into 1½-inch pieces**
- ¼ **cup water**
- 1 **tablespoon unsalted butter**
- ½ **teaspoon table salt**
- ½ **teaspoon minced fresh thyme**
- 1 **tablespoon packed brown sugar**

WHY THIS RECIPE WORKS For a vibrant and nutrient-dense side dish, butternut squash puree fits the bill. It complements just about any roast beautifully but is also at home alongside sautéed chicken or fish. We wanted to avoid having to cook the hard squash on the stove as we knew it would take a while to soften enough to puree in the blender, so we decided to microwave it first for 10 minutes with water, butter, salt, fresh thyme, and a little brown sugar for a touch more sweetness, which worked perfectly. This softened mixture could then be added to the blender jar and pureed on the hard vegetable puree setting, which also heated the mixture. After about 3 minutes, we had just the right mash to which we only needed to add salt and pepper for seasoning.

Microwave all ingredients in covered bowl, stirring occasionally, until squash is softened, about 10 minutes; transfer to Ace blender. Lock lid in place, then select puree program 2 (for hard vegetables). Once program has completed, carefully remove lid and season with salt and pepper to taste. Serve.

SPICED BUTTERNUT SQUASH PUREE
Add ¼ teaspoon cinnamon to bowl with remaining ingredients. Substitute 1 tablespoon maple syrup for sugar.

BUTTERNUT SQUASH PUREE WITH CHIPOTLE AND HONEY
Add 1½ teaspoons minced canned chipotle chile in adobo to bowl with remaining ingredients. Substitute 1 tablespoon honey for sugar.

PARMESAN FARROTTO

SERVES 2 TO 4

TOTAL TIME
45 minutes

1 cup whole farro

1 small onion, chopped fine

3 cups chicken or
vegetable broth

2 tablespoons extra-virgin
olive oil, divided

2 garlic cloves, minced

1 teaspoon minced fresh
thyme or ¼ teaspoon
dried

¼ teaspoon table salt

¼ teaspoon pepper

1 ounce Parmesan cheese,
grated (½ cup)

2 tablespoons minced
fresh parsley

WHY THIS RECIPE WORKS Italian *farrotto* is essentially a risotto-style dish made using farro in place of the usual Arborio rice. Although it is made with a similar method, farro's more robust, nutty flavor gives the dish new dimension. Because much of the starch is trapped inside the outer bran of the farro, achieving a creamy, velvety consistency can be a challenge. Here's where making this dish in a blender is a true advantage. We found that pulsing whole farro just briefly in the blender helped to release its starches for a creamy risotto-like side dish. After pulsing it, we simply added broth along with some finely chopped onion (we didn't want any chunks in our finished dish), fresh thyme, oil, and salt and pepper, and let it all cook and mingle on the blender's chunky soup function. To finish, we added grated Parmesan and more extra-virgin olive oil for flavor and richness and minced parsley for bright flavor. This elegant side dish pairs well with roasted meat, chicken, or fish. We prefer the flavor and texture of whole farro. Do not use quick-cooking, presteamed, or pearled farro (read the ingredient list on the package to determine this) in this recipe. The consistency of farrotto is a matter of personal taste; if you prefer a looser texture, add extra broth before seasoning in step 2.

1. Add farro to Ace blender. Lock lid in place, then process on medium speed until about half of grains are broken into smaller pieces, about 3 seconds. Add onion, broth, 1 tablespoon oil, garlic, thyme, salt, and pepper to blender. Return lid and select soup program 1 (for chunky soups).

2. Once program has completed, carefully remove lid and stir in Parmesan, parsley, and remaining 1 tablespoon oil. Season with salt and pepper to taste. Serve.

DIPS, SPREADS, AND SAUCES AT THE PUSH OF A BUTTON

GREEN GODDESS DIP

SERVES 6 TO 8; MAKES ABOUT 1½ CUPS

TOTAL TIME
10 minutes, plus chilling time

1 tablespoon lemon juice

¼ teaspoon table salt

¼ teaspoon pepper

¼ cup fresh parsley leaves

¼ cup fresh chives, cut into 1½-inch lengths

2 tablespoons fresh tarragon leaves

1 garlic clove, minced

¾ cup mayonnaise

¾ cup sour cream

WHY THIS RECIPE WORKS Green goddess dip is addictive because of its rich creamy texture, hint of tanginess, and abundance of fresh herbs. But how often does anyone have time for the prep work required? And store-bought versions are just not worth the calories. Enter the Ace blender, which makes quick work of turning out this classic dip so you can have it on hand for a crudités platter or make it for a quick snack with cut-up veggies or chips. A combination of equal parts mayonnaise and sour cream made the perfect base for our dip and a wealth of fresh herbs—parsley, chives, and tarragon—added the signature flavors. Since everything was going into the blender there was no need to tediously mince the herbs, which was a great timesaver. A tablespoon of lemon juice added bright flavor and cut through the richness of the dairy. The dip will appear loose right out of the blender but will set up after refrigerating. Serve with rustic bread, pita chips, and/or crudités.

Add all ingredients to Ace blender in order listed. Lock lid in place, then process on medium speed until herbs are finely chopped, about 30 seconds. Transfer dip to serving bowl, cover with plastic wrap, and refrigerate until set and flavors have melded, at least 1 hour or up to 1 day. Season with salt and pepper to taste. Serve.

CHIPOTLE-LIME DIP WITH CILANTRO
Substitute 1 teaspoon grated lime zest plus 1 tablespoon juice for lemon juice and cilantro for parsley. Add 1 tablespoon minced canned chipotle chile in adobo sauce plus ½ teaspoon adobo sauce to blender with remaining ingredients.

FETA-MINT DIP WITH YOGURT
Reduce mayonnaise to ½ cup. Substitute 1 cup plain whole-milk yogurt for sour cream and mint for parsley. Add ½ cup crumbled feta cheese to blender with remaining ingredients.

HERBED SPINACH DIP

SERVES 6 TO 8; MAKES ABOUT 1½ CUPS

TOTAL TIME
15 minutes, plus chilling time

¼ **teaspoon hot sauce**

¾ **teaspoon table salt**

¼ **teaspoon pepper**

10 **ounces frozen chopped spinach, thawed and squeezed dry**

½ **cup fresh parsley leaves**

3 **scallions, cut into 1-inch pieces**

1 **tablespoon chopped fresh dill**

½ **cup sour cream**

½ **cup mayonnaise**

1 **garlic clove, minced**

½ **red bell pepper, stemmed, seeded, and cut into ¾-inch pieces**

WHY THIS RECIPE WORKS You'll find some rendition of spinach dip on just about every potluck table, and one taste is usually enough to make you move along to something else. Most versions just blend some mix of dairy with frozen spinach and often instant soup mix, so it's no wonder they don't have the best flavor. We wanted a dip that was easy to whip up in the blender and emerged bright green, with big spinach flavor and a luxurious, rich texture. A combination of mayonnaise and sour cream created a smooth, creamy base for the dip, while fresh herbs, garlic, and hot sauce replaced soup mix as the flavoring components. A full half cup of parsley leaves brought deep color and herbal undertones to the dip and a little fresh dill added a bright punch of flavor. Scallions added savory notes and chunks of red bell pepper added sweet flavor and a bit of color. Serve with rustic bread, pita chips, and/or crudités.

Add all ingredients to Ace blender in order listed. Lock lid in place and replace lid cap with food tamper. Process on medium speed until herbs and bell pepper are finely chopped and mixture is creamy, about 45 seconds, using tamper as needed to push ingredients towards center of blender jar. Transfer dip to serving bowl, cover with plastic wrap, and refrigerate until flavors have melded, at least 1 hour or up to 1 day. Season with salt and pepper to taste. Serve.

SALSA

SERVES 4 TO 6; MAKES ABOUT 2 CUPS

TOTAL TIME
8 minutes

½ **small red onion, cut into 1-inch pieces**

½ **cup fresh cilantro leaves**

¼ **cup jarred sliced jalapeños**

2 **tablespoons lime juice**

2 **garlic cloves, peeled and chopped**

½ **teaspoon table salt**

1 **(28-ounce) can diced tomatoes, drained**

WHY THIS RECIPE WORKS When it comes to this lively Mexican condiment, the sky is the limit: Salsas can be made from nearly endless combinations of vegetables, fruits, herbs, and spices. And while they are of course great for scooping up with chips or dolloping on tacos, they can also be used as a quick and easy way to bring unexpected, punchy flavors and textures to many other dishes. Classic tomato salsa is only the tip of the iceberg, so it's well worth making at home. For the brightest flavor and the best texture, we eschewed fresh tomatoes (which are inconsistent in both availability and flavor) in favor of always-available canned diced tomatoes (which have both great flavor and texture). Jarred jalapeños proved to be a piquant and convenient flavor booster. We pulsed the ingredients in the blender, then strained the mixture of excess liquid to avoid a soupy salsa.

Add onion, cilantro, jalapeños, lime juice, garlic, and salt to Ace blender. Lock lid in place and replace lid cap with food tamper. Process on medium speed until mixture is finely chopped, about 30 seconds, using tamper as needed to push ingredients toward center of blender jar. Add tomatoes, return lid, and process until combined, about 5 seconds. Drain salsa briefly in fine-mesh strainer, then transfer to serving bowl. Season with salt and pepper to taste. (Salsa can be refrigerated for up to 2 days.)

TOMATO AND BLACK BEAN SALSA
Add ½ teaspoon chili powder to blender with onion. Stir 1 cup canned black beans, rinsed, into salsa before seasoning.

CLASSIC HUMMUS

SERVES 4 TO 6; MAKES ABOUT 1½ CUPS

TOTAL TIME
12 minutes, plus chilling time

- 6 **tablespoons tahini**
- ⅓ **cup water**
- 3 **tablespoons lemon juice**
- 2 **tablespoons extra-virgin olive oil**
- 1 **small garlic clove, peeled and chopped**
- ½ **teaspoon table salt**
- ¼ **teaspoon ground cumin**
- 1 **(15-ounce) can chickpeas, rinsed**

WHY THIS RECIPE WORKS Classic hummus is usually composed of just a few simple ingredients: chickpeas, tahini, olive oil, garlic, and lemon juice. But many traditional recipes can be surprisingly complex, for instance, calling for the chickpeas to be soaked overnight and then skinned. We wanted a simple, streamlined recipe for hummus with a light, silky-smooth texture and a balanced flavor profile. We started with convenient canned chickpeas and got out the Ace blender to make quick work of turning them into a smooth puree. However, when we processed the chickpeas alone, the hummus turned out grainy. We discovered that the key to the best texture was to create an emulsion, so we layered the ingredients into the blender starting with the liquid ingredients and ending with the chickpeas. Earthy cumin kept the flavors balanced. Sprinkle the hummus with a little paprika, if desired, and serve with rustic bread, pita chips, and/or crudités.

1. Add tahini, water, lemon juice, oil, garlic, salt, cumin, and chickpeas to Ace blender (in that order). Lock lid in place, then process on medium speed until chickpeas are fully ground, about 30 seconds. Remove lid and scrape down sides of blender jar. Return lid and process on high speed until smooth, about 1 minute.

2. Transfer hummus to serving bowl, cover with plastic wrap, and let sit at room temperature until flavors meld, about 30 minutes. Serve. (Hummus can be refrigerated for up to 5 days; if necessary, loosen hummus with 1 tablespoon warm water before serving.)

ROASTED RED PEPPER HUMMUS
Omit cumin. Add ¼ cup jarred roasted red peppers, rinsed and patted dry, to blender with chickpeas.

LEMONY HERB HUMMUS
Add 2 tablespoons fresh mint leaves, 1 tablespoon fresh dill fronds, and ¼ teaspoon grated lemon zest to blender with chickpeas.

CLASSIC BASIL PESTO

SERVES 8; MAKES ABOUT 1½ CUPS

TOTAL TIME
20 minutes

¾ cup extra-virgin olive oil, divided

4 garlic cloves, peeled and smashed

½ cup pine nuts

3 cups fresh basil leaves

1 cup fresh parsley leaves

1 tablespoon lemon juice

1 teaspoon table salt

1 ounce Parmesan cheese, grated fine (½ cup)

WHY THIS RECIPE WORKS Pesto is one of the most versatile sauces you can make and dresses up just about anything. It can be prepared with a variety of ingredients—traditionally basil, but also other herbs and greens like parsley and arugula, and even potent ingredients like sun-dried tomatoes or olives. Regardless of the base ingredients, we found there are a few basic requirements to creating a great pesto: Use high-quality extra-virgin olive oil (its flavor really shines through), toast the garlic in the microwave (helps to tame its fiery flavor), and add some type of nuts or seeds (to give the pesto richness and body). When you're tossing the pesto with cooked pasta, it is important to add some pasta cooking water to achieve the proper sauce consistency. This recipe makes enough to sauce 2 pounds of pasta.

1. Microwave 1 tablespoon oil, garlic, and pine nuts in bowl until fragrant, about 30 seconds, stirring halfway through microwaving. Let mixture cool completely, about 10 minutes. Transfer garlic mixture to Ace blender along with remaining 11 tablespoons oil, basil, parsley, lemon juice, and salt. Lock lid in place, then process on medium speed until pesto is smooth and creamy, about 30 seconds.

2. Remove lid, stir in Parmesan, and season with salt and pepper to taste. (Pesto can be refrigerated for up to 3 days or frozen for up to 3 months. To prevent browning, press plastic wrap flush to surface or top with thin layer of olive oil. Bring to room temperature before using.)

ARUGULA AND RICOTTA PESTO

Part-skim ricotta can be substituted here; do not use nonfat ricotta or the pesto will be dry and gummy.

Substitute 2 cups baby arugula for basil and increase parsley to 2 cups. Reduce Parmesan to ¼ cup and stir ⅔ cup whole-milk ricotta cheese into pesto with Parmesan.

MARINARA SAUCE

SERVES 4; MAKES ABOUT 4 CUPS

TOTAL TIME
45 minutes

1 small onion, cut into ¾-inch pieces

3 tablespoons extra-virgin olive oil, divided

2 tablespoons tomato paste

2 garlic cloves, peeled

1 teaspoon table salt

1 (28-ounce) can whole peeled tomatoes

1 teaspoon minced fresh oregano or ¼ teaspoon dried

1 teaspoon sugar, plus extra as needed

2 tablespoons chopped fresh basil

WHY THIS RECIPE WORKS We wanted to make a bright-tasting all-purpose marinara sauce in the blender using just a few pantry ingredients—a sauce we could make while the pasta water boiled and the pasta cooked for a simple weeknight dinner. First, we addressed the all-important aromatic ingredients that would give our sauce its backbone of flavor, namely onion, garlic, and a hefty dose of tomato paste. Just dumping them raw and unbloomed into the blender led to a wan and lackluster marinara—you may as well open a jar of store-bought sauce if you go that route. Instead, blooming the aromatics in the microwave with olive oil rendered them fragrant and more flavorful. Canned whole tomatoes offered reliable bright flavor and optimum texture. We used the program for chunky soups since we like our marinara with some texture, and then we processed the sauce at the end just a bit to thicken it. This recipe makes enough to sauce 1 pound of pasta.

1. Microwave onion, 1 tablespoon oil, tomato paste, garlic, and salt in bowl, stirring occasionally, until onion is softened, about 5 minutes; transfer to Ace blender along with tomatoes and their juice, oregano, and sugar. Lock lid in place, then select soup program 1 (for chunky soups).

2. Once program has completed, process sauce on low speed until slightly thickened but still chunky, about 5 seconds, or thickened and smooth, about 15 seconds. Carefully remove lid and stir in remaining 2 tablespoons oil and basil. Season with salt and pepper to taste. Serve.

APPLESAUCE

SERVES 6 TO 8; MAKES ABOUT 3 CUPS

TOTAL TIME
40 minutes

1½ **pounds Honeycrisp apples, cored and cut into ½-inch pieces**

¾ **cup water**

3 **tablespoons sugar**

⅛ **teaspoon salt**

WHY THIS RECIPE WORKS When we decided to develop a blender applesauce recipe, preserving the taste of fresh apples was paramount. First, we settled on the right apple. We chose Honeycrisp for their balanced sweet-tart flavor and their tendency to break down readily. Second, we learned it was best not to peel the apples; cooking the fruit with the skin on further boosted flavor and the rosy color of the finished applesauce (but you can always peel the apples if you prefer). The chunky soup function cooked the apples perfectly while a quick bit of processing ensured they were properly thickened. We like the flavor of Honeycrisp apples in this recipe, but it will work with other varieties of apples with the exception of Red or Golden Delicious.

1. Add all ingredients to Ace blender. Lock lid in place, then select soup program 1 (for chunky soups).

2. Once program has completed, process applesauce on low speed until slightly thickened but still chunky, about 5 seconds, or thickened and smooth, about 15 seconds. Serve warm or at room temperature. (Apple sauce can be refrigerated for up to 2 days.)

SPICED APPLESAUCE
Substitute packed brown sugar for granulated sugar. Add ¼ teaspoon ground cinnamon to blender with apples.

REFRESHING DRINKS AND SMOOTHIES

SOY MILK

SERVES 4; MAKES 4 CUPS

TOTAL TIME
1 hour 30 minutes, plus
soaking and chilling time

½ **cup dried soybeans,
    picked over and rinsed**

2 **teaspoons sugar**

½ **teaspoon vanilla extract**

⅛ **teaspoon table salt**

WHY THIS RECIPE WORKS Creamy and rich-tasting nondairy soy milk requires only water, dried soybeans, and salt to make. The Ace blender, which has a soy milk button that cooks the soaked soybeans, makes it super easy to turn out a batch with a touch of the button. We think homemade soy milk is far superior to store-bought, which can contain thickeners, emulsifiers, and a great deal of sugar. The neutral palate of soy milk takes well to flavoring so we developed an appealing chocolate variation that uses cocoa powder. Dried soybeans are available at Asian markets, in some well-stocked supermarkets, and online. The longer you soak the soybeans, the richer the milk will be. We found that sugar and vanilla help to round out the flavor of the milk; however, they can be omitted.

1. Place soybeans in bowl and add water to cover by 2 inches. Soak soybeans at room temperature for at least 1 hour or up to 24 hours. Drain and rinse well.

2. Add soaked soybeans, 4½ cups water, sugar, vanilla, and salt to Ace blender. Lock lid in place, then select soy milk program.

3. Once program has completed, set mesh strainer bag included with blender or fine-mesh strainer lined with triple layer of cheesecloth in 4-cup liquid measuring cup. Transfer soybean mixture to prepared strainer and let drain, stirring occasionally, until liquid no longer runs freely and mixture is cool enough to touch, about 30 minutes. Pull edges of strainer bag together and firmly squeeze pulp until liquid no longer runs freely; discard pulp. Transfer milk to airtight container and refrigerate until well chilled, about 1 hour. Serve. (Soy milk can be refrigerated for up to 4 days; stir to recombine before serving.)

CHOCOLATE SOY MILK

Add 2 tablespoons cocoa powder to blender with soybeans.

RICE MILK

SERVES 4; MAKES 4 CUPS

TOTAL TIME
45 minutes, plus chilling time

4 cups water

2 tablespoons long-grain
   white rice, rinsed

2 teaspoons sugar

¾ teaspoon vegetable oil

½ teaspoon vanilla extract

⅛ teaspoon table salt

WHY THIS RECIPE WORKS Rice milk is often thin and watery or thick and starchy. As we discovered, how you handle the rice is the key to a creamy texture. We first tried using soaked rice, but the milk was too thick and tasted cooked. After much testing, we found there was no need to presoak the rice and we used way less than you would expect, just 2 tablespoons. Adding all of the rice to the blender at the beginning along with the other ingredients delivered a rice milk with depth of fresh flavor without becoming gluey. The blender purees everything but we still strain the milk just in case a few granules are left behind. The oil helps to reduce the amount of foam that forms while processing; do not omit it. We found that sugar and vanilla help to round out the flavor of the milk; however, they can be omitted.

1. Add water, rice, sugar, oil, vanilla, and salt to Ace blender. Lock lid in place, then select first rice milk program (for white rice).

2. Once program has completed, strain rice mixture through fine-mesh strainer into bowl, stirring mixture as needed to extract as much liquid as possible. Let cool to room temperature, about 30 minutes. Transfer milk to airtight container and refrigerate until well chilled, about 1 hour. Serve. (Rice milk can be refrigerated for up to 4 days; stir to recombine before serving.)

BROWN RICE MILK
Substitute long-grain brown rice for white rice and select second rice milk program (for brown rice).

ALMOND MILK

SERVES 4; MAKES 4 CUPS

TOTAL TIME
15 minutes, plus chilling time

4 cups water

5 ounces blanched slivered
or sliced almonds

2 teaspoons sugar

½ teaspoon vanilla extract

⅛ teaspoon table salt

WHY THIS RECIPE WORKS Much of the almond milk available in stores is loaded with thickeners, stabilizers, and gums. We wanted a simple recipe for almond milk that tasted great and would be easy to whip up in our blender. During our tests making the milk, we discovered it was not necessary to soak the nuts ahead of time, making preparation even easier. We tested several ratios of almonds to water to determine which produced both the best flavor and the best texture. We found that blending 5 ounces soaked almonds with 4 cups of water gave us the ideal flavor and consistency. We then poured the mixture through a cheesecloth-lined fine-mesh strainer to separate the almond milk from the pulp. Since the pulp still contained a great deal of milk, we squeezed the pulp in the cheesecloth until no liquid remained. An equal amount of whole blanched almonds can also be used; however, they should be soaked in water for at least 1 hour or up to 24 hours before using. We found that sugar and vanilla help to round out the flavor of the milk; however, they can be omitted.

1. Add water, almonds, sugar, vanilla, and salt to Ace blender. Lock lid in place, then select nut/oat milk program.

2. Once program has completed, set mesh strainer bag included with blender or fine-mesh strainer lined with triple layer of cheesecloth in 4-cup liquid measuring cup. Transfer almond mixture to prepared strainer and let drain, stirring occasionally until liquid no longer runs freely, about 2 minutes. Pull edges of strainer bag together and firmly squeeze pulp until liquid no longer runs freely; discard pulp. Transfer milk to airtight container and refrigerate until well chilled, about 1 hour. Serve. (Almond milk can be refrigerated for up to 4 days; stir to recombine before serving.)

SPICED ALMOND MILK
Add 1 teaspoon ground cinnamon and 1 teaspoon vanilla extract to blender with water.

OAT MILK

SERVES 4; MAKES 4 CUPS

TOTAL TIME
15 minutes, plus chilling time

4 cups water

¾ cup old-fashioned rolled oats

2 teaspoons sugar

¾ teaspoon vegetable oil

½ teaspoon vanilla extract

⅛ teaspoon table salt

WHY THIS RECIPE WORKS Oat milk is quickly becoming one of the most popular alternative milks because of its nutritional profile and the fact that it is also soy, nut, and gluten free (as long as you use oats processed in a gluten-free facility). It's cheap to make and also super easy, so what's not to love about having it on hand to add to your favorite smoothies or just drink straight from the fridge? And you can feel good about drinking oat milk because it is high in iron and oats are known to boost immunity and lower cholesterol. Quick-cooking rolled oats can be substituted, if necessary; do not substitute steel-cut oats. Avoid squeezing the oat pulp too firmly; it will cause the milk to be starchy. The oil helps to reduce the amount of foam that forms while processing; do not omit it. We found that sugar and vanilla help to round out the flavor of the milk; however, they can be omitted.

1. Add water, oats, sugar, oil, vanilla, and salt to Ace blender. Lock lid in place, then select nut/oat milk program.

2. Once program has completed, set mesh strainer bag included with blender or fine-mesh strainer lined with triple layer of cheesecloth in 4-cup liquid measuring cup. Transfer oat mixture to prepared strainer and let drain, stirring occasionally, until liquid no longer runs freely, about 5 minutes. Pull edges of strainer bag together and firmly squeeze pulp until liquid no longer runs freely; discard pulp. Transfer milk to airtight container and refrigerate until well chilled, about 1 hour. Serve. (Oat milk can be refrigerated for up to 4 days; stir to recombine before serving.)

OAT MILK WITH GINGER AND TURMERIC
Add 1 teaspoon grated fresh ginger and ¼ teaspoon ground turmeric to blender with water.

MIXED BERRY SMOOTHIES

SERVES 2 TO 4; MAKES ABOUT 3 CUPS

TOTAL TIME
8 minutes

¼ **cup orange juice**

¾ **cup plain yogurt**

⅛ **teaspoon table salt**

1 **ripe banana, peeled and
cut into 1-inch pieces**

12 **ounces (2¼ cups) frozen
mixed berries**

WHY THIS RECIPE WORKS The key to making a good smoothie is to get the proportion of ingredients just right. We like to use yogurt as the base of our fruit smoothies because it helps to ensure a rich but drinkable texture while also adding a bit of welcome tang to balance out the sweetness of the fruit. We also replaced the ice called for in most smoothie recipes with frozen fruit. We found that ice diluted the smoothies too much and that frozen fruit, flash-frozen at its peak ripeness, provided the most consistent results. We love using Greek yogurt in the test kitchen, but for these smoothies we preferred plain regular yogurt because of its looser texture. We added ⅛ teaspoon of salt, which helped bring out the fruit's overall flavor. We like the simplicity of using frozen mixed berries, but you can substitute any combination of berries as long as it equals 12 ounces.

Add all ingredients to Ace blender in order listed. Lock lid in place and replace lid cap with food tamper. Select smoothie program and use tamper as needed to push ingredients toward center of blender jar. Serve.

TROPICAL FRUIT SMOOTHIES
Substitute 6 ounces frozen mango chunks and 6 ounces frozen pineapple chunks for mixed berries and pineapple juice for orange juice.

PEACH-STRAWBERRY SMOOTHIES
Substitute 6 ounces frozen strawberries and 6 ounces frozen peaches for mixed berries.

GREEN SMOOTHIES

SERVES 2 TO 4; MAKES ABOUT 3 CUPS

TOTAL TIME
8 minutes

- 1 cup water
- ½ cup pineapple juice
- ⅛ teaspoon table salt
- 1 cup baby kale
- 1 ripe banana, peeled and cut into 1-inch pieces
- ½ ripe avocado, pitted and cut into quarters
- 2 tablespoons hemp seed hearts
- 1 cup frozen pineapple chunks

WHY THIS RECIPE WORKS A feel-good "green" smoothie with kale and pineapple tasted great while also making us feel virtuous. For a creamy texture, rich, nutritious, and subtly sweet avocado fit the bill. We tried every protein add-in imaginable, from commonly used almond butter to the new and novel, like cannellini beans. We wanted something that packed a nutritional punch but wouldn't overwhelm the flavor of our smoothies. Unsurprisingly, the beans made our smoothies taste bland and starchy. Almond butter and wheat germ were good, but we ultimately came away with a new favorite that worked with any flavor combination we threw at it: hemp seed hearts. The hulled center of the hemp seed is a soft, almost waxy nugget, which blended beautifully into our drink, leaving just a trace of pleasantly grassy, sweet flavor. We like the neutral flavor and color of hemp seed hearts, but you can use 2 tablespoons almond butter or ¼ cup wheat germ in its place. You can find hemp seed hearts in the natural foods section of most well-stocked supermarkets. Do not use frozen chopped kale for this recipe.

Add all ingredients to Ace blender in order listed. Lock lid in place and replace lid cap with food tamper. Select smoothie program and use tamper as needed to push ingredients toward center of blender jar. Serve.

WATERMELON-LIME AGUAS FRESCAS

SERVES 8 TO 10; MAKES ABOUT 8 CUPS

TOTAL TIME
8 minutes

8 cups seedless watermelon,
   cut into 1-inch pieces

2 cups water

⅓ cup lime juice (3 limes),
   plus extra as needed

2 tablespoons agave
   nectar or honey, plus
   extra as needed

⅛ teaspoon table salt

   Mint leaves (optional)

WHY THIS RECIPE WORKS *Agua fresca*, meaning "fresh water," is the catchall term for a wide variety of popular nonalcoholic beverages made by combining fruits, grains, seeds, or flowers with sugar and water. These drinks are served from large barrel-style glass jars and make for a very colorful and appealing display. One of our favorites is a version made with watermelon. The method was simple enough; we processed the melon and water in our blender and then strained out the pulp. We accented our agua fresca with fresh lime juice for a light tang, and just a bit of agave nectar and a little salt brought out all the sweet and tart flavors in the drink.

Working in 2 batches, process watermelon and water in Ace blender on high speed until smooth, about 30 seconds. Strain mixture through fine-mesh strainer into 2-quart pitcher; discard solids. Stir lime juice, agave, and salt into watermelon mixture. Season with extra lime juice and agave to taste. Serve over ice, garnished with mint, if using. (Agua fresca can be refrigerated for up to 5 days; stir to recombine before serving.)

FROZEN MARGARITAS

SERVES 4; MAKES ABOUT 6 CUPS

TOTAL TIME
10 minutes

- ¼ **cup kosher salt (optional)**
- 1 **lime wedge, plus extra for garnishing**
- ⅔ **cup blanco or reposado tequila**
- ¼ **cup orange liqueur**
- 1 **(12-ounce) container frozen limeade concentrate**
- 5 **cups (20 ounces) ice cubes**

WHY THIS RECIPE WORKS If you only know a margarita to be the sickly sweet, too-icy machine slush that is often offered up at many a Tex-Mex restaurant, get ready for a revelation. Our frozen version has tangy, true citrus flavor and a perfect semifrozen consistency. Rather than squeezing, sweetening, and freezing juice from fresh limes, we opted for the convenience of frozen limeade concentrate (made from real limes), which offered the ideal sweet-tart balance. We then tested our way to the best and most balanced proportions of citrus and alcohol: 3 parts limeade concentrate to 2 parts tequila and orange liqueur combined. Blending in ice cubes ensured the optimum frozen texture.

1. Spread salt into even layer on small plate, if using. Rub outside rims of 4 chilled old-fashioned or margarita glasses with lime wedge to moisten, then dip rims into salt to coat. Set glasses aside.

2. Add tequila, orange liqueur, limeade concentrate, and ice to Ace blender (in that order) and process on high speed until smooth, about 1 minute, scraping down sides of blender jar as needed. Divide margarita between prepared glasses and garnish with extra lime wedges before serving.

FROZEN PIÑA COLADAS

SERVES 4; MAKES ABOUT 6 CUPS

TOTAL TIME
8 minutes

- 2 tablespoons sugar
- 2 tablespoons warm tap water
- 1 (15-ounce) can coconut cream
- ⅔ cup white rum
- 12 ounces frozen pineapple
- 2 cups (8 ounces) ice cubes

WHY THIS RECIPE WORKS We wanted to create a frozen piña colada bursting with real tropical fruit flavor. With that in mind, we first compared fresh pineapple, frozen pineapple, canned pineapple, and pineapple juice. Tasters found the natural flavor of fresh pineapple more appealing than the processed flavor of canned or juice. Since we were making a frozen drink, frozen pineapple (fresh fruit frozen at its peak of ripeness) offered the best of both worlds, providing the flavor of fresh while reducing the amount of additional ice needed for texture. Next we experimented with cream of coconut, coconut milk, and coconut cream. Many recipes call for cream of coconut, but tasters thought this made the drink taste like sunblock and coconut milk was too thin and watery. We ultimately picked coconut cream for its great mouthfeel and rich, natural coconut flavor. As for the rum, choosing from the array of colors and grades was no easy task (though it was a fun one). White rum provided just the right flavor, holding its own with the pineapple and coconut without overpowering them. Do not substitute cream of coconut for the coconut cream, as the former is heavily sweetened and the latter is not. Garnish with fresh pineapple slices, pineapple leaves, and cocktail cherries, if desired.

Whisk sugar and water together in small bowl until sugar has dissolved. Add sugar syrup, coconut cream, rum, pineapple, and ice to blender (in that order) and process on high speed until smooth, about 1 minute, scraping down sides of blender jar as needed. Divide piña colada between chilled old-fashioned or hurricane glasses and serve.

NO-FUSS DESSERTS AND FROZEN TREATS

VANILLA MILKSHAKES

SERVES 2 TO 4

TOTAL TIME
20 minutes

4 cups vanilla ice cream

½ cup milk

Pinch table salt

WHY THIS RECIPE WORKS Milkshakes are a perennial favorite, and it's no wonder: A thick, creamy milkshake is an indulgent treat for kids and adults alike. To re-create a classic diner shake at home, we found it was best to use the smoothie mode on the blender. Its powerful bursts of blending (in conjunction with occasional stirring with the food tamper) break up softened ice cream and combine it with milk to create a thick but pourable milkshake. To amp up the vanilla flavor in our milkshake, we added a pinch of salt, which also offset the sweetness. For a chocolate version, we turned to cocoa powder (chocolate sauce was much too sweet), and added malted milk powder for complex, well-rounded flavor. Serving these milkshakes in chilled glasses helps them stay colder longer. Our favorite vanilla ice cream is Turkey Hill Original Vanilla Premium Ice Cream.

Let ice cream sit at room temperature to soften slightly, about 15 minutes. Place milk, ice cream, and salt in Ace blender (in that order). Lock lid in place and replace lid cap with food tamper. Select smoothie program and use tamper as needed to push ingredients towards center of blender jar. Serve in chilled glasses.

MALTED CHOCOLATE MILKSHAKES
Add ¼ cup malted milk powder and 1 tablespoon unsweetened cocoa powder to blender with other ingredients.

NO-CHURN VANILLA ICE CREAM

SERVES 4 TO 6; MAKES ABOUT 1 QUART

TOTAL TIME
8 minutes, plus freezing time

2 **cups heavy cream**

1 **cup sweetened condensed milk**

¼ **cup whole milk**

¼ **cup light corn syrup**

2 **tablespoons sugar**

1 **tablespoon vanilla extract**

¼ **teaspoon table salt**

WHY THIS RECIPE WORKS For this easy-to-make version of vanilla ice cream, we created a rich ice cream base by first blending heavy cream to whip and aerate it. Then we added the rest of the ingredients, including sweetened condensed milk, which added not only sweetness but also body to the finished ice cream. A generous dose of vanilla extract provided rich vanilla flavor. Bypassing the churning step, we placed the mixture in the freezer for 6 hours before serving. We prefer to chill the cream mixture in a loaf pan to ensure it freezes quickly, but an 8-inch square baking pan will also work.

1. Add cream to Ace blender. Lock lid in place, then process on medium speed until soft peaks form, about 30 seconds. Remove lid and scrape down sides of blender jar. Return lid and continue to process until stiff peaks form, about 10 seconds. Using rubber spatula, stir in condensed milk, whole milk, corn syrup, sugar, vanilla, and salt. Process until thoroughly combined, about 20 seconds, scraping down sides of blender jar as needed.

2. Pour cream mixture into 8½ by 4½-inch loaf pan and smooth into even layer. Press plastic wrap flush against surface of cream mixture and freeze until firm, at least 6 hours or up to 5 days. Serve.

NO-CHURN MILK CHOCOLATE ICE CREAM
Reduce vanilla to 1 teaspoon. Add 6 ounces melted, cooled milk chocolate to blender with condensed milk.

NO-CHURN PEACH COBBLER ICE CREAM
Omit sugar. Substitute 1 tablespoon bourbon for vanilla. Add ½ cup peach preserves and ¼ teaspoon ground cinnamon to blender with condensed milk. After transferring cream mixture to loaf pan, gently stir in ½ cup coarsely chopped shortbread cookies before covering and freezing.

BANANA ICE CREAM

SERVES 4 TO 6; MAKES ABOUT 1 QUART

TOTAL TIME
20 minutes, plus freezing time

6 **very ripe bananas**

½ **cup heavy cream**

1 **tablespoon vanilla extract**

1 **teaspoon lemon juice**

¼ **teaspoon table salt**

¼ **teaspoon ground cinnamon**

WHY THIS RECIPE WORKS For a lighter alternative to classic ice cream that still had all the creaminess and flavor of the real thing, we turned to a pair of secret weapons: bananas and our blender. Bananas were a perfect choice for our ice cream base: Their high pectin content allows them to remain creamy when frozen. We started by simply slicing whole, frozen, peeled bananas and then pureeing them in the blender. Letting the bananas come to room temperature for 15 minutes before slicing made them easier to cut and process. The end result had good banana flavor, but it wasn't quite as creamy as tasters wanted. We decided to try adding a little dairy to help achieve our desired consistency. We tested banana ice creams made with both milk and heavy cream; the version made with just a half cup of heavy cream produced an unbeatable silky-smooth texture. Ripe, heavily speckled (or even black) bananas contain plenty of sweetness, so we skipped additional sugar. We did, however, add a bit of lemon juice, vanilla, and cinnamon to give our ice cream more dimension. We prefer to chill the banana mixture in a loaf pan to ensure it freezes quickly, but an 8-inch square baking pan will also work.

1. Peel bananas, place in large zipper-lock bag, and press out excess air. Freeze bananas until solid, at least 8 hours.

2. Let bananas sit at room temperature to soften slightly, about 15 minutes, then slice into ½-inch-thick rounds. Add cream, vanilla, lemon juice, bananas, salt, and cinnamon to Ace blender (in that order). Lock lid in place and replace lid cap with food tamper. Select ice cream program and use tamper as needed to push ingredients toward center of blender jar.

3. Transfer banana mixture to 8½ by 4½-inch loaf pan and smooth into even layer. Press plastic wrap flush against surface of mixture and freeze until firm, at least 6 hours or up to 5 days. Serve.

PEANUT BUTTER–BANANA ICE CREAM
Reduce heavy cream to ¼ cup. Add ¼ cup peanut butter to blender with bananas.

GRAPEFRUIT-ELDERFLOWER SORBET

SERVES 4 TO 6; MAKES ABOUT 1 QUART

TOTAL TIME
10 minutes, plus freezing time

2¼ **cups grapefruit juice (3 grapefruits)**

¾ **cup water**

½ **cup sugar**

2 **tablespoons elderflower liqueur (optional)**

WHY THIS RECIPE WORKS Sorbets are a fresh, light ending to a meal and are a snap to make using fruit juice, a few other ingredients, and your blender. (Normally you need fresh fruit and an ice cream maker to get the right texture.) And once you have the sorbet formula down, you can vary it endlessly, even turning out grown-up versions like this one that's flavored with elderflower liqueur. We simply poured the liquid mixture into two ice cube trays; when the cubes had hardened we pulsed them using the ice cream function, which broke them up most effectively. Then we refroze the slushy mixture for just the right texture for our sorbet. We found that processing the frozen cubes in two smaller batches rather than a single large batch made for more even blending. Our favorite brand of grapefruit juice is Natalie's 100% Florida Grapefruit Juice. We prefer to chill the sorbet mixture in a loaf pan to ensure it freezes quickly, but an 8-inch square baking pan will also work.

1. Whisk grapefruit juice, water, sugar, and elderflower liqueur, if using, together in bowl until sugar has dissolved. Pour mixture into 2 ice cube trays and freeze until firm, about 4 hours.

2. Place half of frozen cubes in Ace blender. Lock lid in place and replace lid cap with food tamper. Select ice cream program and use tamper as needed to push ingredients toward center of blender jar.

3. Transfer grapefruit mixture to 8½ by 4½-inch loaf pan and smooth into even layer; transfer to freezer. Repeat processing with remaining cubes; transfer to loaf pan and smooth into even layer. Press plastic wrap flush against surface of mixture and freeze until firm, at least 6 hours or up to 5 days. Serve.

PINEAPPLE-RUM SORBET
Substitute pineapple juice for grapefruit juice and aged rum for elderflower liqueur.

ORANGE-CAMPARI SORBET
Substitute orange juice for grapefruit juice and Campari for elderflower liqueur.

DARK CHOCOLATE MOUSSE

SERVES 4

TOTAL TIME
10 minutes, plus chilling time

- 4 ounces bittersweet or semisweet chocolate, chopped fine
- 3 tablespoons water
- 1 tablespoon unsweetened cocoa powder
- 1½ teaspoons sugar
- ½ teaspoon instant espresso powder (optional)
- Pinch table salt
- ¾ cup heavy cream

WHY THIS RECIPE WORKS There are many ways to make an ethereal chocolate mousse, but our eggless blender version is perhaps the easiest. First we melted dark chocolate in the microwave along with water, cocoa powder, sugar, and espresso powder (which deepens the chocolate flavor). Then to lighten the mixture and give it the right mousse-like texture, we whipped an abundance of heavy cream right in the blender until stiff peaks formed, then processed it a bit further after adding the melted chocolate mixture. This mousse is denser and richer than those containing egg whites, but has plenty of aeration from the whipped cream. Our favorite bittersweet chocolate is Ghirardelli 60% Cacao Bittersweet Chocolate Premium Baking Bar. If you make the mousse more than a day in advance, we recommend letting it sit at room temperature for 10 minutes before serving. Serve with whipped cream and chocolate shavings, if desired.

1. Microwave chocolate, water, cocoa, sugar, espresso powder, if using, and salt in bowl at 50 percent power, stirring occasionally, until melted, 2 to 4 minutes; set aside.

2. Add cream to Ace blender. Lock lid in place, then process on medium speed until stiff peaks form, about 30 seconds. Remove lid and scrape down sides of blender jar with rubber spatula. Add chocolate mixture, return lid, and process on medium speed until almost completely combined (a few streaks of whipped cream will remain on sides of jar), about 10 seconds. Stir mousse by hand to incorporate remaining whipped cream.

3. Portion mousse into 4 individual serving dishes. Cover with plastic wrap and refrigerate until set, at least 4 hours or up to 2 days. Serve.

MIXED BERRY MOUSSE

SERVES 4

TOTAL TIME
45 minutes, plus chilling time

20 **ounces (4 cups) thawed frozen blackberries, blueberries, raspberries, and/or strawberries**

6 **tablespoons sugar, divided**

1 **teaspoon finely grated lemon zest**

Pinch table salt

1½ **teaspoons unflavored gelatin**

½ **cup heavy cream**

3 **ounces cream cheese, softened**

WHY THIS RECIPE WORKS There's a good reason berry mousse recipes aren't that prevalent: Berries contain lots of juice, and that can ruin the texture of a delicate mousse, which should be creamy and rich. Plus, the fruit flavor produced by most recipes is too subtle. To tackle these challenges and create a truly bright, flavorful mousse, we started by macerating frozen berries with sugar, lemon zest, and a little salt. This caused the berries to release their liquid, which we strained out. We then mixed 3 tablespoons of the drained juice with gelatin to thicken our mousse. Reducing the rest of the berry liquid in the microwave and adding it to the gelatin mixture boosted the concentrated berry flavor. Next, we fully pureed the juiced berries, which added a lot of fresh berry flavor. Finally, we added cream cheese, an unusual addition for mousse, for a creamier body and half a cup of heavy cream for richness. The whole thing whipped up into a perfectly smooth mousse right in the blender. For an even smoother mousse, you can strain the berry puree in step 3 through a fine-mesh strainer before processing with the remaining ingredients. If you make the mousse more than a day in advance, we recommend letting it sit at room temperature for 10 minutes before serving. Serve with whipped cream and fresh berries, if desired.

1. Combine berries, 3 tablespoons sugar, lemon zest, and salt in bowl and let sit for 30 minutes, stirring occasionally.

2. Strain berries through fine-mesh strainer over separate bowl; transfer berries to Ace blender and set aside. Transfer 3 tablespoons drained juice into small bowl, sprinkle gelatin over top, and let sit until gelatin softens, about 5 minutes. Meanwhile, microwave remaining juice until reduced to 3 tablespoons, 4 to 5 minutes. Whisk gelatin mixture and remaining 3 tablespoons sugar into reduced juice until dissolved.

3. Lock blender lid in place, then process berries on medium speed until smooth, about 30 seconds. Add gelatin mixture, heavy cream, and cream cheese to blender, return lid, and process on medium speed until combined, about 10 seconds. Increase speed to high and process until smooth, about 30 seconds, pausing to scrape down sides of blender jar as needed.

4. Portion mousse into 4 individual serving dishes. Cover with plastic wrap and refrigerate until set, at least 4 hours or up to 2 days. Serve.

NUTRITIONAL INFORMATION

To calculate the nutritional values of our recipes per serving, we used The Food Processor SQL by ESHA Research. When using this program, we entered all the ingredients, using weights for important ingredients such as most vegetables. We also used our preferred brands in these analyses. We did not include additional salt or pepper for food that's "seasoned to taste." If there is a range in the serving size, we used the highest number of servings to calculate the nutritional values.

	Calories	Total Fat (G)	Sat Fat (G)	Chol (MG)	Sodium (MG)	Total Carbs (G)	Fiber (G)	Sugar (G)	Protein (G)
PERFECT SOUPS WITHOUT THE STOVETOP									
Classic Chicken Noodle Soup	180	2.5	0.5	45	750	16	2	4	22
Chicken and Ramen Soup	360	12	4.5	45	2030	33	2	4	30
Mexican Chicken Soup	170	2	0	30	660	20	3	4	18
Beef and Barley Soup	190	6	1	40	690	16	3	3	18
Spaghetti and Meatball Soup	210	7	2	15	1170	23	2	5	12
Creamy Tomato Soup	180	11	7	30	1120	16	2	11	4
Carrot-Ginger Soup	120	3	2	10	1070	19	5	10	5
Butternut Squash Soup	150	6	3.5	15	730	24	4	7	2
Super Greens Soup	180	8	1.5	0	990	20	3	4	8
Corn Chowder	250	10	4.5	30	690	33	2	6	9
Loaded Baked Potato Soup	320	17	11	55	560	32	2	3	12
Black Bean Soup	170	4.5	0.5	0	940	27	9	4	9
Hearty White Bean Soup with Sausage and Cabbage	190	9	2.5	25	970	19	5	5	11
Red Lentil Soup with North African Spices	250	5	0.5	0	810	38	9	4	14
EASY MAINS AND SIDES YOU'RE SURE TO ACE									
Chicken Cacciatore	200	4	1	60	920	14	3	8	25
Chicken Tagine with Chickpeas and Apricots	300	7	1	45	950	37	7	22	23
Mole Chicken Tacos	610	19	3	120	780	59	3	16	53
Easy Ground Beef Chili	270	11	2.5	35	1350	26	8	8	19
Sweet and Sour Beef with Shiitakes and Bell Pepper	260	7	2	70	630	22	1	16	27
Barbecued Pork Sandwiches	570	21	4	90	1070	62	0	37	30

	Calories	Total Fat (G)	Sat Fat (G)	Chol (MG)	Sodium (MG)	Total Carbs (G)	Fiber (G)	Sugar (G)	Protein (G)
EASY MAINS AND SIDES YOU'RE SURE TO ACE (cont.)									
Thai Shrimp Curry	340	23	19	145	630	15	2	6	20
Indian Vegetable Curry	200	5	0.5	0	1010	30	8	5	10
Zoodles Puttanesca	210	14	1.5	0	650	19	4	11	6
Creamy Mashed Cauliflower	80	3.5	2	10	360	11	5	4	4
Butternut Squash Puree	90	0	0	0	300	23	3	7	2
Parmesan Farrotto	290	11	2	5	660	39	1	4	12
DIPS, SPREADS, AND SAUCES AT THE PUSH OF A BUTTON									
Green Goddess Dip	170	19	4	20	210	1	0	1	1
Herbed Spinach Dip	130	13	2.5	10	380	3	1	1	2
Salsa	180	0	0	0	2580	38	11	17	6
Classic Hummus	180	14	2	0	330	10	3	0	5
Classic Basil Pesto	270	28	4	5	360	3	1	0	4
Marinara Sauce	160	11	1.5	0	1070	13	2	8	2
Applesauce	60	0	0	0	40	15	2	13	0
REFRESHING DRINKS AND SMOOTHIES									
Soy Milk	100	4.5	0.5	0	75	7	2	2	8
Rice Milk	90	1	0	0	75	18	0	0	2
Almond Milk	210	18	1.5	0	75	8	4	2	7
Oat Milk	70	1.5	0	0	75	13	2	0	2
Mixed Berry Smoothies	100	1.5	1	5	95	20	4	13	3
Green Smoothies	140	6	1	0	95	21	4	8	3
Watermelon-Lime Aguas Frescas	50	0	0	0	30	13	1	11	1
Frozen Margaritas	260	0	0	0	5	40	0	36	0
Frozen Piña Coladas	530	17	16	0	40	74	1	63	2
NO-FUSS DESSERTS AND FROZEN TREATS									
Vanilla Milkshakes	290	16	10	60	160	33	0	29	6
No-Churn Vanilla Ice Cream	510	34	21	110	200	46	0	46	7
Banana Ice Cream	180	7	4.5	25	105	30	3	16	2
Grapefruit-Elderflower Sorbet	100	0	0	0	0	25	0	17	0
Dark Chocolate Mousse	310	28	17	50	50	19	2	3	3
Mixed Berry Mousse	330	18	11	60	125	39	4	32	4

CONVERSIONS AND EQUIVALENTS

Some say cooking is a science and an art. We would say that geography has a hand in it, too. Flours and sugars manufactured in the United Kingdom and elsewhere will feel and taste different from those manufactured in the United States. So we cannot promise that the loaf of bread you bake in Canada or England will taste the same as a loaf baked in the States, but we can offer guidelines for converting weights and measures. We also recommend that you rely on your instincts when making our recipes. Refer to the visual cues provided. If the dough hasn't "come together in a ball" as described, you may need to add more flour—even if the recipe doesn't tell you to. You be the judge.

The recipes in this book were developed using standard U.S. measures following U.S. government guidelines. The charts below offer equivalents for U.S. and metric measures. All conversions are approximate and have been rounded up or down to the nearest whole number.

EXAMPLE

1 teaspoon = 4.9292 milliliters, rounded up to 5 milliliters

1 ounce = 28.3495 grams, rounded down to 28 grams

VOLUME CONVERSIONS

U.S.	METRIC
1 teaspoon	5 milliliters
2 teaspoons	10 milliliters
1 tablespoon	15 milliliters
2 tablespoons	30 milliliters
¼ cup	59 milliliters
⅓ cup	79 milliliters
½ cup	118 milliliters
¾ cup	177 milliliters
1 cup	237 milliliters
1¼ cups	296 milliliters
1½ cups	355 milliliters
2 cups (1 pint)	473 milliliters
2½ cups	591 milliliters
3 cups	710 milliliters
4 cups (1 quart)	0.946 liter
1.06 quarts	1 liter
4 quarts (1 gallon)	3.8 liters

WEIGHT CONVERSIONS

OUNCES	GRAMS
½	14
¾	21
1	28
1½	43
2	57
2½	71
3	85
3½	99
4	113
4½	128
5	142
6	170
7	198
8	227
9	255
10	283
12	340
16 (1 pound)	454

INDEX

Note: Page references in *italics* indicate photographs.